At Issue

Superbugs

Other Books in the At Issue Series

At Issue

| Superbugs

Tamara Thompson, Book Editor

GREENHAVEN PRESS
A part of Gale, Cengage Learning

GALE
CENGAGE Learning

Farmington Hills, Mich • San Francisco • New York • Waterville, Maine
Meriden, Conn • Mason, Ohio • Chicago

Judy Galens, *Manager, Frontlist Acquisitions*

© 2016 Greenhaven Press, a part of Gale, Cengage Learning.

Gale and Greenhaven Press are registered trademarks used herein under license.

For more information, contact:
Greenhaven Press
27500 Drake Rd.
Farmington Hills, MI 48331-3535
Or you can visit our Internet site at gale.cengage.com

ALL RIGHTS RESERVED.
No part of this work covered by the copyright herein may be reproduced, transmitted, stored, or used in any form or by any means graphic, electronic, or mechanical, including but not limited to photocopying, recording, scanning, digitizing, taping, Web distribution, information networks, or information storage and retrieval systems, except as permitted under Section 107 or 108 of the 1976 United States Copyright Act, without the prior written permission of the publisher.

For product information and technology assistance, contact us at

Gale Customer Support, 1-800-877-4253
For permission to use material from this text or product, submit all requests online at www.cengage.com/permissions.

Further permissions questions can be e-mailed to permissionrequest@cengage.com.

Articles in Greenhaven Press anthologies are often edited for length to meet page requirements. In addition, original titles of these works are changed to clearly present the main thesis and to explicitly indicate the author's opinion. Every effort is made to ensure that Greenhaven Press accurately reflects the original intent of the authors. Every effort has been made to trace the owners of copyrighted material.

Cover image copyright © Images.com/Corbis.

LIBRARY OF CONGRESS CATALOGING-IN-PUBLICATION DATA

Superbugs / Tamara Thompson, book editor.
    pages cm. -- (At issue)
  Summary: "Books in Greenhaven Press's At Issue series focus a wide range of viewpoints onto a single controversial issue, providing in-depth discussions by leading advocates, a quick grounding in the issues, and a challenge to critical thinking skills."-- Provided by publisher.
  Includes bibliographical references and index.
  ISBN 978-0-7377-7388-0 (hardback) -- ISBN 978-0-7377-7389-7 (paperback)
  1. Drug resistance in microorganisms--Juvenile literature. 2. Business ethics. 3. Bacteria--Juvenile literature. I. Thompson, Tamara, editor.
  QR177.S87 2016
  616.9'041--dc23616.9'041--dc23
                 2015031227

Printed in Mexico
1 2 3 4 5 6 7 20 19 18 17 16

Contents

Introduction

Imagine falling from a skateboard and skinning a knee or cutting a toe on a broken piece of glass while going barefoot in the summer. No big deal, right? A little antibiotic ointment and a bandage and everything will be fine after a few days. But increasingly, that isn't how it works out.

Instead, people with routine wounds and illnesses caused by bacteria are sometimes developing drug-resistant infections that can't be knocked out, even by the strongest modern antibiotics. They end up suffering organ damage, losing limbs, and sometimes even their lives. And the problem is likely to get a lot worse before it gets better, experts say.

One of the oldest forms of life on the planet and also the most numerous, bacteria are microscopic single-cell organisms that are found everywhere on earth—in soil, water, air, and on and in the bodies of animals, including humans, where they help digest food and fight infection and disease. Life couldn't exist without bacteria, but not all types are beneficial and some are downright deadly. For example, the Black Death plague in the Middle Ages, which killed an estimated seventy-five million to two hundred million people (30 to 60 percent of Europe's population), was caused by bacteria likely transmitted to humans by rats. No one knew how to cure it because bacteria hadn't even been discovered yet.

Medical science has progressed light years since then, however, beginning with the discovery of germ theory in 1676, which established that diseases are caused by microorganisms too small to see, including bacteria. The development of the first antibiotic—a substance that kills bacteria—didn't come until 1928, when the discovery of penicillin ushered in a new age of medical progress. Today there are dozens of classes of powerful antibiotics developed to target specific types of bacteria.

Before the use of antibiotics, simple cuts and illnesses caused by bacteria (such as urinary tract infections and pneumonia) were often fatal, and surgeries and dental procedures that are now routine were often deadly as well. Antibiotics are the key factor that allowed modern medicine to become the effective system it is today, with low mortality rates and positive outcomes for many if not most procedures. Lifesaving antibiotics have been the cornerstone of modern medical treatment for nearly a century, but that is rapidly changing, experts say.

In recent decades, many antibiotics have stopped working; but the drugs aren't growing weaker, the bacteria are growing stronger. The overuse and misuse of antibiotics in humans and livestock is one key factor in the development of so-called superbugs, bacteria that have become resistant to antibiotic medications. That happens when bacteria are exposed to antibiotics that don't entirely kill them off, instead making them resistant to future encounters with the drug and others like it. This can happen when people take antibiotics unnecessarily, or when they begin antibiotic treatment but do not finish all of their medicine.

While hospitals remain the primary source of superbug infections, especially the most dangerous ones, some types of resistant bacteria are also finding their way into the general population. The superbug MRSA, for example, is a strain of staph bacteria that has become resistant to a drug called methicillin, and others related to it, including penicillin. MRSA is now commonly found in American homes as well as such places as day care centers, gyms, jails, and other sites where people congregate. MRSA can still be treated with other antibiotics, but the drug options are dwindling and the infections are hard to fight; they sometimes lead to necrotizing fasciitis, a condition that destroys body tissue, which is why newspaper headlines sometimes refer to MRSA as the "flesh-eating bacteria."

According to the US Centers for Disease Control and Prevention, more than two million Americans get sick with drug-resistant superbug infections each year, and a shocking twenty-three thousand die because there are no effective antibiotics left to treat their specific bacterial conditions.

A 2014 report by the British government warns that a postantibiotic world without drugs to fight common infections and diseases could be just around the corner. By 2050, the report estimates, more than ten million people will die globally each year due to antibiotic resistance, up from an estimated eight hundred thousand today. That's more than the current worldwide deaths from cancer, diabetes, and cholera combined. The World Health Organization has also sounded the alarm, calling for antibiotic resistance to become an urgent global priority.

Although there is broad consensus about the severity of the emerging superbug crisis, there is also broad finger-pointing when it comes to assigning blame for the cause.

The medical profession has acknowledged that the way antibiotics have been used is at the core of the problem and is taking steps to reduce the use of antibiotics and improve sanitation protocols; but increasing public awareness is key to curtailing the overuse of drugs that millions of Americans have become accustomed to taking when sick with ailments such as sinus infections and strep throat.

Another factor that experts say contributes to antibiotic resistance is the longstanding practice of routinely feeding low doses of antibiotics to healthy food animals, such as chickens, pigs, and cows, to prevent disease and promote weight gain. Experts have known since the mid-1970s that the practice leads to bacteria that are resistant to the drugs—both in animals and humans—but the agriculture industry has dismissed the claim for decades.

Every year since 2007, microbiologist and congressional representative Louise Slaughter, a Democrat from New York, has introduced legislation to phase out the use of eight classes of medically important antibiotics in food animals that are not sick, but her bills have been stalled each time due to pressure from the farming and pharmaceutical industries, who still maintain that the practice is both safe and necessary.

But that may be changing, too. As public awareness of the issue grows and consumers increasingly demand antibiotic-free meat options, factory farms are beginning to reduce their use of the drugs in healthy animals. Whether such baby steps will make a difference remains to be seen.

Regardless of where one places the blame for antibiotic resistance, one thing is clear: superbugs must be stopped or a century of medical progress could be lost and the world may find itself with as few options to stop infections as were available back in the Middle Ages—none.

"People aren't going to be able to have their teeth fixed, or their hip replaced, if we don't stop this," Representative Slaughter told *Healthline* in 2014. "All of the new medicine, all of the new surgeries, the basis of that being successful is antibiotic use. We're talking about strep throat being fatal. That's the scariest thing."[1]

The authors in *At Issue: Superbugs* present a wide range of viewpoints that examine how bacteria develop drug resistance, the factors contributing to their spread, and what can or should be done to halt the growing global superbug crisis.

---

1. Quoted in Brian Krans, "How Lethal Bacteria Evolve to Survive," *Healthline*, July 24, 2014. http://www.healthline.com/health/antibiotics/resistance-basics.

How Lethal Bacteria Evolve to Survive

Brian Krans

Brian Krans is an award-winning investigative reporter and co-founder of the web-based news service Healthline News.

Bacteria are single-cell organisms that serve a variety of important functions in the human body, from aiding in the digestion of food to helping fight off infection and disease. Humans cannot exist without bacteria, but some strains of it are deadly in their own right, while others have become potentially so because they have developed a resistance to modern antibiotics. Experts are alarmed at how quickly this has happened and say that unless changes are made to the way antibiotics are used, these lifesaving drugs may become useless to the point where common medical problems become life-or-death situations. Some twenty-three thousand Americans die each year from untreatable bacterial infections, a number that is expected to grow sharply if antibiotic-resistant bacteria continue to develop and spread.

Earlier this year [2014], Dr. Neil Fishman faced a tough decision. A 54-year-old man fell off his roof while doing housework, injuring his leg. Six months later, bacteria resistant to most antibiotics had infected the wound. Fishman, associate chief medical officer for the University of Pennsylvania

Brian Krans, "How Lethal Bacteria Evolve to Survive," healthline.com, July 24, 2014. Copyright © 2014 Healthline Networks, Inc. All rights reserved. Reproduced with permission.

Health System, saw few choices: use an old, toxic antibiotic that didn't work well and would destroy the patient's kidneys, or amputate his leg.

"It's scary to me that in 2014 those are the only two options to give him," Fishman, who is also chair of the Society of Healthcare Epidemiology of America's Education & Research Foundation, told Healthline.

The patient had his leg amputated, thus saving his life. That case is anything but isolated. Fishman has been working on antibiotic resistance since the early 1990s, and has watched along with other infectious disease experts as deadly bacteria have grown stronger, antibiotic use has increased, and new antibiotic discovery has fallen to an all-time low.

It has been 86 years since the first antibiotic was discovered. Experts like Fishman can cite reams of scientific evidence that show antibiotics are not as safe as they were once thought to be, and that widespread, indiscriminate antibiotic use triggers antibiotic resistance and other complications.

The discovery of antibiotics made all medical procedures less risky, but they are slowly losing their effectiveness.

"They're the only drug where administration to one patient can affect another person," Fishman said.

But how do single-celled organisms continue to outsmart the species that put men on the moon and robots on Mars? The short answer is that they've been doing it since long before we learned to walk on two feet.

An Emerging Epidemic in the 21st Century

The discovery of antibiotics made all medical procedures less risky, but they are slowly losing their effectiveness.

Bacteria are everywhere. And in most cases, that's a good thing. Those tiny, single-celled organisms are keeping you alive by helping you digest your meals and aiding your body in fighting off infection and disease. Scientists at the National Institutes of Health are isolating and mapping the genes of all these bacteria, collectively called the human microbiome.

They're strong, resourceful, and plentiful. Microbes outnumber us by 10,000,000,000,000,000,000,000 to 1, they have existed 1,000 times longer than *Homo sapiens*, and they are capable of creating 500,000 generations in one human's lifetime.

While humans simply can't exist without the help of bacteria, many strains are deadly and have been the source of billions of deaths throughout history.

Humans were given a leg up when Dutch scientist Antonie van Leeuwenhoek discovered bacteria under a microscope in 1676, and one better when Alexander Fleming discovered penicillin in 1928. Those discoveries have led to the development of dozens of classes of antibiotics.

These drugs have been so crucial for so long that we've nearly forgotten what it's like when common medical problems become life-or-death situations, though the signs of a reversal have been there all along.

Those who have been studying the issue, from top U.S. government infectious-disease scientists to doctors fighting to save their patients' lives, say we need to quit our old habits and get with the new science. According to the World Health Organization, we aren't far from a world where our best defenses against bacteria are rendered useless.

Rep. Louise Slaughter, D-N.Y., the only microbiologist in Congress, has repeatedly and unsuccessfully tried to change the way America uses antibiotics since 2007.

"People aren't going to be able to have their teeth fixed, or their hip replaced, if we don't stop this. All of the new medicine, all of the new surgeries, the basis of that being successful is antibiotic use," she told Healthline. "We're talking about strep throat being fatal. That's the scariest thing."

The Greatest Bacterial Threats Facing the United States

The CDC says 23,000 Americans die every year from untreatable bacterial infections.

Bacteria have always had the ability to evolve defenses against organisms designed to kill them. In fact, microbes, including bacteria, are the most abundant and toughest forms of life on our planet.

Bacteria that had been isolated from the earth's surface for more than four million years have been discovered in the depths of Lechuguilla Cave in New Mexico.

Some of these single-celled organisms have become so tough that we now call them "superbugs" because they can outsmart our best antibiotic defenses. And 23,000 Americans die each year because of them.

A recent study in the *Journal of the Pediatric Infectious Diseases Society* found that antibiotic-resistant bacteria are on the rise, especially in children ages 1 to 5. While a large number of infections occur inside the healthcare system, these children infected with drug-resistant bacteria had limited exposure to hospitals. And nearly three-quarters of the bacteria studied produced an enzyme that made them resistant to multiple classes of antibiotics.

Bacteria that had been isolated from the earth's surface for more than four million years have been discovered in the depths of Lechuguilla Cave in New Mexico. Researchers found that those bacteria were highly resistant to as many as 14 different commercially available antibiotics.

"This supports a growing understanding that antibiotic resistance is natural, ancient, and hard wired in the microbial pangenome," the researchers wrote in the journal *PLOS One*.

Before the discovery of antibiotics, routine surgeries, cuts, and diseases caused by bacteria were often fatal. For example, tuberculosis (TB)—caused by the bacterium *Mycobacterium tuberculosis*—killed millions of people all over the world each year. The development of the antibiotic streptomycin in 1943 reduced the fatality rate for this common bacterial infection by 90 percent.

But TB hasn't gone away. Multidrug-resistant TB—those strains that are resistant to the drugs isoniazid and rifampin—increased after a resurgence in 1992, are widespread in some developing countries, and still hospitalized 72 Americans in 2012.

The Top Three Threats

Drug-resistant TB is only one of the threats identified by the U.S. Centers for Disease Control and Prevention (CDC). The top three are:

- *Clostridium difficile (C. diff)*: populates a person's gut and can cause lethal diarrhea

- *Carbapenem-resistant Enterobacteriaceae* (CRE): nicknamed the "nightmare bacteria" because this family of bacteria is fatal in half of all cases

- Drug-resistant *Neisseria gonorrhoeae*: a species of bacteria responsible for the sexually transmitted infection gonorrhea, which can cause infertility in young women

While these are the biggest threats, recent research published in the journal *Current Biology* found that bacteria all over the world—on nearly every surface—have the ability to become antibiotic resistant. The most abundant and diverse pool of resistance was found in soil, where bacteria possessed genes resistant to vancomycin, tetracycline, or beta-lactam antibiotics.

All three are commonly used in veterinary and human medicine. The overuse of antibiotics was something Fleming warned about after discovering penicillin more than eight decades ago.

"It is not difficult to make microbes resistant to penicillin in the laboratory by exposing them to concentrations not sufficient to kill them, and the same thing has occasionally happened in the body," he wrote while accepting the Nobel Prize in 1945. "The time may come when penicillin can be bought by anyone in the shops. Then there is the danger that the ignorant man may easily underdose himself and by exposing his microbes to non-lethal quantities of the drug, make them resistant."

We're dangerously close to what the world looked like before the discovery of penicillin.

While you can't buy over-the-counter antibiotics at your neighborhood pharmacy, they are available at animal-feed stores. The widespread use of antibiotics in animals and humans has public health officials sounding the alarm that something must change.

"We are literally running out of antibiotics. We're seeing more and more germs that our current antibiotics can't treat," Fishman said. "We're dangerously close to what the world looked like before the discovery of penicillin."

How Bacteria Evolve to Survive

Superbugs can learn how to outsmart antibiotics, including by eating their dead.

The most common way bacteria develop drug resistance is through lateral gene transfer, in which bacteria pass information to one another like a student passing a note in class.

Dr. Karl Klose of the University of Texas at San Antonio explained this phenomenon during a TEDx talk: "This is equivalent of you going to the funeral of someone who had blue eyes, taking a piece of their body out of the casket, and eating it. And hey! You have blue eyes too. But now imagine that instead of blue eyes, you now are resistant to tetracycline."

Bacteria can also transfer genes using viruses, direct contact, and good old-fashioned reproduction. While it can take decades to develop a new antibiotic, bacteria can evolve around one in as little as 20 minutes.

Dr. John Bolton, clinical professor of pediatrics at the University of California, San Francisco, said it's basic biology that the easiest way to develop antibiotic resistance is to administer low doses of antibiotics over a long period of time, much like how antibiotics are used in animal feed. "It's a scary situation, and we've known about it for 40 to 50 years," he said.

Using Antibiotics in Livestock

The animals we eat are fed a steady diet of antibiotics, in part because it fattens them up.

Agriculture accounts for 80 percent of all antibiotics used in the U.S., and there's continued pressure from interested parties to maintain the status quo.

As of 2011, about 80 percent of all swine farms, cattle feedlots, and sheep farms reported that they use low levels of antibiotics in feed and water for growth or health purposes, according to the Department of Agriculture's Animal and Plant Health Inspection Service.

Antibiotics become less effective the more often they're used.

Carmen Cordova, a microbiologist with the Natural Resources Defense Council, said emerging science shows how antibiotic use in animals affects human health. She said studies now show how *staphylococcus aureus*, one type of staph bacteria, can be present in humans, transferred through close contact to pigs, where it picks up resistance to the antibiotics in their feed, and then re-entered into the human population through pork consumption.

"The risks were acknowledged 40 years ago. What's changed is that now you have more solid evidence. You have more sophisticated ways to show this is happening," Cordova told Healthline. "The studies that are coming out now are really solid, concrete pieces of evidence that can really put this picture together."

More Antibiotics Makes Things Worse

Public health campaigns encourage doctors to use good judgment.

Antibiotics become less effective the more often they're used, and *C. diff* is one example of how this occurs. While scientists once thought antibiotics were the cure for this stomach infection, experts now know they are actually the cause.

Drug-resistant *C. diff* infections—which account for 12 percent of all hospital-acquired infections—occur when beta-lactam antibiotics clear the gut of other bacteria, allowing *C. diff* to flourish and cause potentially fatal diarrhea.

The way *C. diff* infections work is only one discovery that is leading scientists to believe antibiotics aren't as safe as once thought. The most widespread overuse of antibiotics in humans is as a treatment for the common cold. As viruses—not bacteria—are the cause of colds, administering antibiotics does nothing but give bacteria ample experience to outsmart the drugs and potentially cause unwanted side effects such as vomiting and diarrhea.

"We've been trusted with these antibiotics that have been developed over decades and we need to preserve their effectiveness for the future," Dr. Tom Frieden, CDC director, warned in September. "More medication isn't better. The right medications are better. It is not too late. If we're not careful, the medicine chest will be empty."

The CDC and other major health organizations have launched public-awareness campaigns urging patients and doctors to be judicious with using antibiotics because the CDC has presented evidence that slowing prescribing rates is directly linked to fewer drug-resistant bacteria.

Ramanan Laxminarayan, director and senior fellow at the Center for Disease Dynamics, Economics & Policy, said that we need a seismic shift in how antibiotics are handled in order to slow the oncoming epidemic.

"We need to stop thinking of antibiotics as commodities and more as resources," he told Healthline.

The Overuse of Antibiotics in Humans Creates Drug-Resistant Superbugs

National Institutes of Health

Founded in 1887, the National Institutes of Health (NIH) is one of the world's foremost medical research centers and the federal focal point for medical research in the United States. NIH comprises twenty-seven separate institutes and centers that conduct research in different disciplines of biomedical science. It is one of eight health agencies of the Public Health Service, which in turn is part of the US Department of Health and Human Services.

In recent decades, many antibiotics have stopped working; but the drugs aren't growing weaker, the bacteria are growing stronger. The overuse and misuse of antibiotics in humans is a key factor in the development of superbugs, bacteria that have become resistant to antibiotic medications. This happens when bacteria are exposed to antibiotics that don't entirely kill them off, instead making them resistant to future encounters with the drug and others like it. This can happen when people take antibiotics unnecessarily or when they begin antibiotic treatment but do not finish all of their medicine. Experts say antibiotics should only be used when absolutely necessary and that good sanitation can help prevent many bacterial infections in the first place.

National Institutes of Health, "Stop the Spread of Superbugs: Help Fight Drug-Resistant Bacteria," *NIH News in Health*, February 2014. Courtesy of NewsinHealth.nih.gov. All rights reserved. Reproduced with permission.

For nearly a century, bacteria-fighting drugs known as antibiotics have helped to control and destroy many of the harmful bacteria that can make us sick. But in recent decades, antibiotics have been losing their punch against some types of bacteria. In fact, certain bacteria are now unbeatable with today's medicines. Sadly, the way we've been using antibiotics is helping to create new drug-resistant "superbugs."

Superbugs are strains of bacteria that are resistant to several types of antibiotics. Each year these drug-resistant bacteria infect more than 2 million people nationwide and kill at least 23,000, according to the U.S. Centers for Disease Control and Prevention (CDC). Drug-resistant forms of tuberculosis, gonorrhea, and staph infections are just a few of the dangers we now face.

Antibiotics are among the most commonly prescribed drugs for people. They're also given to livestock to prevent disease and promote growth. Antibiotics are effective against bacterial infections, such as strep throat and some types of pneumonia, diarrheal diseases, and ear infections. But these drugs don't work at all against viruses, such as those that cause colds or flu.

Unfortunately, many antibiotics prescribed to people and to animals are unnecessary. And the overuse and misuse of antibiotics helps to create drug-resistant bacteria.

Here's how that might happen. When used properly, antibiotics can help destroy disease-causing bacteria. But if you take an antibiotic when you have a viral infection like the flu, the drug won't affect the viruses making you sick. Instead, it'll destroy a wide variety of bacteria in your body, including some of the "good" bacteria that help you digest food, fight infection, and stay healthy. Bacteria that are tough enough to survive the drug will have a chance to grow and quickly multiply. These drug-resistant strains may even spread to other people.

Too Much of a Good Thing

Over time, if more and more people take antibiotics when not necessary, drug-resistant bacteria can continue to thrive and spread. They may even share their drug-resistant traits with other bacteria. Drugs may become less effective or not work at all against certain disease-causing bacteria.

You can help slow the spread of drug-resistant bacteria by taking antibiotics properly and only when needed.

"Bacterial infections that were treatable for decades are no longer responding to antibiotics, even the newer ones," says Dr. Dennis Dixon, an NIH expert in bacterial and fungal diseases. Scientists have been trying to keep ahead of newly emerging drug-resistant bacteria by developing new drugs, but it's a tough task.

"We need to make the best use of the drugs we have, as there aren't many in the antibiotic development pipeline," says Dr. Jane Knisely, who oversees studies of drug-resistant bacteria at NIH. "It's important to understand the best way to use these drugs to increase their effectiveness and decrease the chances of resistance to emerge."

You can help slow the spread of drug-resistant bacteria by taking antibiotics properly and only when needed. Don't insist on an antibiotic if your health care provider advises otherwise. For example, many parents expect doctors to prescribe antibiotics for a child's ear infection. But experts recommend delaying for a time in certain situations, as many ear infections get better without antibiotics.

The Spread of MRSA

NIH researchers have been looking at whether antibiotics are effective for treating certain conditions in the first place. One recent study showed that antibiotics may be less effective than previously thought for treating a common type of sinus infection. This kind of research can help prevent the misuse and overuse of antibiotics.

"Treating infections with antibiotics is something we want to preserve for generations to come, so we shouldn't misuse them," says Dr. Julie Segre, a senior investigator at NIH. In the past, some of the most dangerous superbugs have been confined to health care settings. That's because people who are sick or in a weakened state are more susceptible to picking up infections. But superbug infections aren't limited to hospitals. Some strains are out in the community and anyone, even healthy people, can become infected.

When antibiotics are needed, doctors usually prescribe a mild one before trying something more aggressive like vancomycin.

One common superbug increasingly seen outside hospitals is methicillin-resistant *Staphylococcus aureus* (MRSA). These bacteria don't respond to methicillin and related antibiotics. MRSA can cause skin infections and, in more serious cases, pneumonia or bloodstream infections.

A MRSA skin infection can appear as one or more pimples or boils that are swollen, painful, or hot to the touch. The infection can spread through even a tiny cut or scrape that comes into contact with these bacteria. Many people recover from MRSA infections, but some cases can be life-threatening. The CDC estimates that more than 80,000 aggressive MRSA infections and 11,000 related deaths occur each year in the United States.

When antibiotics are needed, doctors usually prescribe a mild one before trying something more aggressive like vancomycin. Such newer antibiotics can be more toxic and more expensive than older ones. Eventually, bacteria will develop resistance to even the new drugs. In recent years, some superbugs, such as vancomycin-resistant *Enterococci* bacteria, remain unaffected by even this antibiotic of last resort.

"We rely on antibiotics to deliver modern health care," Segre says. But with the rise of drug-resistant bacteria, "we're running out of new antibiotics to treat bacterial infections," and some of the more potent ones aren't working as well.

Slow Test Results

Ideally, doctors would be able to quickly identify the right antibiotic to treat a particular infection. But labs need days or even weeks to test and identify the bacteria strain. Until the lab results come in, antibiotic treatment is often an educated guess.

"We need to know how to treat for a favorable outcome, but knowledge about the infection can be several days away," explains Dr. Vance Fowler, an infectious disease expert at Duke University School of Medicine.

Fowler says faster diagnostic testing offers one of the best hopes for treating infectious diseases. Technology is catching up, he says, and new research in this area looks promising.

Genetic studies by NIH-supported researchers such as Segre and Fowler are also helping us understand the unique characteristics of antibiotic-resistant bacteria. Their findings could point the way to innovative new treatments.

While scientists search for ways to beat back these stubborn bacteria, you can help by preventing the spread of germs so we depend less on antibiotics in the first place.

The best way to prevent bacterial infections is by washing your hands frequently with soap and water. It's also a good idea not to share personal items such as towels or razors. And use antibiotics only as directed. We can all do our part to fight drug-resistant bacteria.

Tips for Blocking Harmful Bacteria

- Wash your hands often with soap and water, or use an alcohol-based hand sanitizer.

- If you're sick, make sure your doctor has a clear understanding of your symptoms. Discuss whether an antibiotic or a different type of treatment is appropriate for your illness.

- If antibiotics are needed, take the full course exactly as directed. Don't save the medicine for a future illness, and don't share with others.

- Maintain a healthy lifestyle—including proper diet, exercise, and good hygiene—to help prevent illness, thereby helping to prevent the overuse or misuse of medications.

Routine Antibiotic Use in Animal Feed Is a Major Cause of Superbugs

Barry Estabrook

Barry Estabrook is a two-time winner of the prestigious James Beard Foundation Award for food writing and author of the book Tomatoland, *a look at how industrial agriculture has changed one of America's favorite foods.*

Experts have known since the mid-1970s that regularly feeding farm animals low doses of antibiotics leads to bacteria that are resistant to the drugs—both in animals and in humans—but the agriculture industry dismissed the claims for decades. It is becoming increasingly harder to do so, however, as numerous studies confirm that the superbug problem is worse than feared. Nevertheless, more antibiotics are fed to livestock than ever before, and not just for the treatment of disease but also for disease prevention and to promote growth. A coalition of groups has sued the Food and Drug Administration to halt the nontherapeutic use of two important human antibiotics in animal feed, but both the farm and pharmaceutical industries still maintain the practice is not dangerous to humans.

Stuart Levy once kept a flock of chickens on a farm in the rolling countryside west of Boston. No ordinary farmer, Levy is a professor of molecular biology and microbiology and of medicine at Tufts University School of Medicine. This

Barry Estabrook, "You Want Superbugs With That?," onearth.org, May 27, 2011. Copyright © 2011 On Earth. All rights reserved. Reproduced with permission.

was decades ago, and his chickens were taking part in a never-before-conducted study. Half the birds received feed laced with a low-dose of antibiotics, which U.S. farmers routinely administer to healthy livestock—not to cure illness, but merely to increase the animals' rates of growth. The other half of Levy's flock received drug-free food.

Results started showing up almost instantly. Within two days, the treated animals began excreting feces containing *E. coli* bacteria that were resistant to tetracycline, the antibiotic in their feed. (*E. Coli*, most of which are harmless, normally live in the guts of chickens and other warm-blooded animals, including humans.) After three months, the chickens were also excreting bacteria resistant to such potent antibiotics as ampicillin, streptomycin, carbenacillin, and sulfonamides. Even though Levy had added only tetracycline to the feed, his chickens had somehow developed what scientists now call "multidrug resistance" to a host of antibiotics that play important roles in treating infections in people. More frightening, although none of the members of the farm family tending the flock were taking antibiotics, they, too, soon began excreting drug-resistant strains of *E. coli*.

Proponents of growth promotion keep asking for more data, and we scientists provide them. But then the findings have never led to removal of the practice.

When Levy's study was published in *The New England Journal of Medicine* in 1976, it was met with skepticism. "The other side—industry—could not believe that this would have happened. The mood at the time was that what happens in animals does not happen in people," said Levy, who serves as president of the Alliance for the Prudent Use of Antibiotics, in a telephone interview from his office at Tufts. "But we had the data. It was obvious to us even then that using antibiotics this way was an error and should be stopped."

Use in Livestock Thrives

During the intervening 35 years, study after study has confirmed Levy's findings and shown that the problem of antibiotic-resistant "superbugs" is even worse than anyone could have imagined. . . . And even as the number of infectious diseases is on the rise, more antibiotics are administered to livestock than ever before, from 17.8 million pounds per year in 1999 according to the Animal Health Institute (a trade organization of companies, like Bayer, Novartis, and Pfizer, that manufacture livestock drugs) to 29.8 million pounds in 2009, according to the U.S. Food and Drug Administration, or FDA. Fully 80 percent of the antibiotics used in the United States are given to livestock, and the vast majority are administered to promote growth and stave off potential infections, not to treat illness.

From his perspective of more than three decades as a resistant-microbe watcher, Levy sounded almost weary when he said, "Proponents of growth promotion keep asking for more data, and we scientists provide them. But then the findings have never led to removal of the practice."

Earlier this week [May 2011], the Natural Resources Defense Council, Center for Science in the Public interest, Food Animal Concerns Trust, Public Citizen, and the Union of Concerned Scientists joined forces to file a lawsuit against the FDA. The groups want the agency to withdraw its approval for most non-therapeutic uses of penicillin and tetracycline in animal feed. They say that it's something regulators should have done decades ago.

A Long History

The FDA first approved the use of low-dose antibiotics in the 1950s. Concerns about the drugs began appearing within a decade, and by the time Levy's paper was published, the FDA was aware the practice posed a serious risk to human health. The agency proposed to withdraw its approval in 1977, saying that new evidence showed that penicillin- and tetracycline-containing products had not been "shown safe for widespread, sub-therapeutic use."

The proposal drew howls of outrage from two of the most powerful lobbying groups in Washington, agribusinesses and drug manufacturers. Both the House and Senate ordered the FDA to "hold in abeyance any and all implementation of the proposal" until further studies had been conducted. "It was the power of the lobby and the money behind that lobby," Levy recalled.

Exposure to even miniscule levels of drugs equips bacteria with the genetic resilience to fend off higher levels of the same drugs.

As requested by Congress, the FDA commissioned three studies during the 1980s, all of which supported initial concerns about the risks of feeding farm animals antibiotics on a daily basis. The FDA received petitions urging it to act from coalitions of scientific and environmental groups in 1999 and 2005. Such respected bodies as the American Academy of Pediatrics, the Centers for Disease Control and Prevention, the National Academy of Sciences, the U.S. Department of Agriculture, and the World Health Organization all identified low-dose antibiotics as the reason antibiotic-resistant bacteria were proliferating in humans and animals. And the FDA—which is charged with protecting the health of Americans—failed to act, only going so far as to issue a "Draft Guidance" report and a draft "Action Plan" proposing voluntary guidelines. These suggestions have done nothing to stem the deluge of unnecessary antibiotics through the spigot of agribusiness.

"We've been fighting the non-therapeutic use of antibiotics in livestock for more than 30 years," Margaret Mellon, director of the food and environment program at the Union of Concerned Scientists, said in a press release announcing the lawsuit. "And over those decades the problem has steadily worsened. We hope this lawsuit will finally compel the FDA to act with an urgency commensurate with the magnitude of the problem." (Siobhan Delancey, a spokeswoman for the FDA, declined to comment on the suit.)

The Trouble with Antibiotics

Bacteria are evolutionary dynamos. Untold trillions of them can live in one confined animal feeding operation, or CAFO—the technical term for a factory farm. They breed rapidly and mutate readily. Exposure to even miniscule levels of drugs equips bacteria with the genetic resilience to fend off higher levels of the same drugs.

From the dawn of modern antibiotics, researchers have been aware that the seeds of the wonder drugs' destruction had already been sown. In his 1945 Nobel acceptance speech for his discoveries related to penicillin, Sir Alexander Fleming said, "There is a danger that the ignorant man may easily under-dose himself and by exposing his microbes to non-lethal quantities of the drug make them resistant." Fleming's prediction was prescient—except the problem wasn't an "ignorant man" but politicians and business executives whose priorities lay elsewhere.

During the decades that the FDA dithered, a mountain of scientific research accumulated showing that antibiotic-resistant bacteria can not only evolve in the guts of farm animals, but can spread from animals to the humans who tend them, and then be passed on to people who have never been anywhere near a chicken house or hog barn.

What the Dutch Discovered

In 2004, Dutch doctors discovered a strain of methicillin-resistant *Staphylococcus aureus* (MRSA) in a six-month-old baby. Often fatal, MRSA is the original "superbug" because it can survive treatment by the most powerful antibiotics in modern medicine's arsenal. At first, the doctors were puzzled. MRSA was primarily known as a hospital-acquired infection. But the child, who carried the germs but never became sick, as is often the case with the asymptomatic carriers of bacteria, had never been in a hospital. Her parents were pig farmers, and subsequent investigations showed that the MRSA had been passed from the pigs to the parents and on to the baby. (Most bacteria are non-infectious, although they may carry resistance genes. The problem is that they can pass their resistance traits to infectious bacteria.)

There are any number of ways antibiotic resistant bacteria can spread from farm to fork.

Three years later, J. Scott Weese, a professor at the Ontario Veterinary College at the University of Guelph near Toronto, found an identical strain of MRSA in Canadian pigs and their owners. The superbug had somehow leapt over the Atlantic Ocean. Further research by Weese revealed that the swapping of resistant bacteria between animals and humans can be a two-way street. Not only were the farmers affected by MRSA that had originated in pigs, but the pigs carried MRSA that until then had only been found in humans.

"A Problem That Couldn't Happen Here"

For a year or so, American agribusiness continued to claim that MRSA was a problem that couldn't happen here—a myth they were able to perpetate because no government agency was routinely testing hogs for MRSA. But during the summer of 2008, Tara Smith, a microbiologist at the University of Iowa and the deputy director of the university's Center for Emerging Infectious Diseases, found that seven out of ten pigs she and her students tested on farms in Illinois and Iowa carried MRSA.

A graduate student working with Smith recently uncovered a strain of *S. aureus* associated with hogs and the people who tend them in a day care worker who had never been near a hog farm. Fortunately, that particular strain was not antibiotic resistant. But the discovery showed that humans do not have to work with infected animals to pick up the bacteria they carry. "Whether the pig bacterium was passed on via another human or via contaminated food products, we can't tell right now," Smith said in an email.

Making the Case

In fact, there are any number of ways antibiotic resistant bacteria can spread from farm to fork. A recently published study in the journal *Clinical Infectious Diseases* found that 47 percent of the beef, chicken, pork, and turkey sampled from grocery stores in five U.S. cities carried drug-resistant *S. aureus*. Superbugs are literally blowing in the wind. According to a 2006 report in the journal *Environmental Health Perspectives*, multi-drug resistant bacteria were found in the air downwind of a confined hog operation. Nearly 90 percent of the *E. coli* in liquid manure pits associated with pig farms are resistant to drugs, according to Kellogg Schwab, the director of the Johns Hopkins Center for Water and Health. Manure ponds frequently burst their banks and contaminate nearby streams, rivers, and wells.

Pharmaceutical companies dispute the assertion that treating animals with low-dose antibiotics is dangerous to humans. "A lot of people want to talk about antibiotic resistance as if it is a big amorphous issue," said Ron Phillips of the Animal Health Institute, in an interview. "It is, in fact, a series of discrete issues where you have to look at specific bug/drug combinations and figure out what are the potential pathways for antibiotic-resistant material to transfer from animals to humans. Studies have been done, and have come to the conclusion that there is a vanishingly small level of risk."

Smith of the University of Iowa says that the specific studies that the industry suggests are necessary simply cannot be done—it would be the equivalent of having to have an eyewitness to prosecute any crime. "But we have DNA from the crime scene that matches that of the suspect. At some point you have to accept that he is responsible. The bulk of evidence is overwhelming."

FDA figures show that 60 percent of the antimicrobial drugs [drug companies] sell are fed to farm animals to promote growth, an enormous chunk of their business.

Would Industry-Wide Changes Help?

One area where solid scientific evidence is lacking, astonishingly, is on whether changing the industry-wide practice of giving low doses of antibiotics to livestock would actually make that much of a difference. The experience of farmers in the European Union, where dosing animals with sub-therapeutic levels of antibiotics was banned in 1998, suggests otherwise. Denmark is the world's largest pork exporting country, and most of its hogs are raised in large confined operations much like those used by the U.S. pork industry. In that country, the overall use of antibiotics fell by 37 percent between 1994 and 2009, according to a study by Denmark's National Food Institute. Correspondingly, levels of resistant bacteria in animals and people plummeted, but production levels of meat either stayed the same or increased: The average daily weight gain per pig was actually higher in 2008 than in 1992 when antibiotics were routinely administered.

It's easy to understand why drug companies react so forcefully to any attempts to cut back on sub-therapeutic antibiotic use—FDA figures show that 60 percent of the antimicrobial drugs they sell are fed to farm animals to promote growth, an enormous chunk of their business—but given the success of farmers in Europe who've stopped using antibiotics to promote growth, why is the farm lobby so vehemently against change? Would it spell the end of the huge CAFOs upon which American agribusiness has come to depend? Steven Roach, the public health program director for the Food Animal Concerns Trust (FACT), one of the plaintiffs in the lawsuit against the FDA, has a straightforward answer to that question: No, CAFOs would not go away. European pig farms are as large as those in the U.S., according to Roach. Some of the E.U.'s chicken operations are even larger than those in this country. (And if American farmers feel uncomfortable with examples from foreign countries, he suggests that they look at Tyson, one of the United States' largest poultry producers, which had no problems raising chickens without antibiotics in ways that the suit aims to stop.)

Doing Without

"There are two parts of production where there are small economic benefits to using low-dose antibiotics," Roach said in an interview. "Particularly on young pigs. The challenge for the beef cattle industry is that when you feed a high-corn diet, cattle have some heath problems, and one way they manage that is using the antibiotics in the feed. But even so, some producers are raising them without antibiotics in feedlots now." Roach said that European farmers have gotten around these problem areas by weaning piglets later. Barns are kept cleaner for all animals. And altering diets allows CAFOs to raise cattle without antibiotics. Of course, says Roach, some farmers simply won't want to change. He believes they are afraid that if they allow outside forces to impose even small changes, then other changes are bound to come.

After 35 years on the frontlines in the battle to keep antibiotics effective, though, Levy believes there's cause for optimism. "The mood is now 180 degrees better than it was for getting rid of this practice," he said. "There are more and more scientists and lay people who are urgently asking for an end to this use of antibiotics."

Science in Congress

It helps that one of those "science people" is also a congresswoman. Louise Slaughter, a Democrat who represents upstate New York, was a microbiologist before going into politics. In 2009, she introduced a bill called the Preservation of Antibiotics for Medical Treatment Act, which calls for the FDA to withdraw its approval of the practice within two years unless there is reasonable certainty that the low-dose antibiotics cause no harm to human health. "We are witnessing a looming public health crisis that is moving from farms to grocery stores to dinner tables around the country," she said in an email. "As the only microbiologist in Congress, I feel it's my duty to bring public attention to this."

Although Slaughter's bill has yet to pass, it had 127 cosponsors in the last Congressional session, more than double its support in the previous Congress. It looks as though even more legislators will sign on this time, and many are hopeful that the combined forces of looming legislation and an active lawsuit will finally lead the FDA to act. "If we don't address it," Slaughter continued, "we risk setting ourselves back to the time before antibiotics, when even common infections could kill a person. That's not any kind of world I want my children and their children to inherit."

L.W. Nixon Library
Butler Community College
901 South Haverhill Road
El Dorado, Kansas 67042-3280

Antibiotics in Animal Feed Are Not to Blame for Superbugs

Richard Raymond

Food safety and public health consultant Richard Raymond was the undersecretary for food safety at the US Department of Agriculture from 2005 to 2008. He practiced family medicine in Nebraska for twenty-seven years before entering public service.

Agriculture is unfairly getting the blame for the rise of antibiotic-resistant superbugs. Not only is the use of antibiotics in animals misrepresented with badly skewed statistics, but most of the drugs fed to animals aren't even important in human medicine. The use of antibiotics in food animals is not the main driver of antibiotic resistance; unwise use in humans is. The US government should not further restrict the use of antibiotics in food animals because it will lead to more sick animals and raise the cost of meat. Medically important antibiotics need to be protected, but the effort should focus on human use, not use in the food industry.

From what I have been reading lately, it appears to me that the next big fight over agriculture's ability to provide consumers with plentiful, safe and affordable meat and poultry products will focus on the use of antibiotics in animals raised for food.

Richard Raymond, "Antibiotics and Animals Raised for Food: Lies, Damn Lies and Statistics," *Food Safety News*, January 7, 2013. FoodSafetyNews.com. Copyright © 2013 Food Safety News. All rights reserved. Reproduced with permission. Subtitles have been added for clarity.

And it also appears to me that the information being provided through media outlets is not designed to inform, but to misinform and play on the public's lack of detailed knowledge about the use of antibiotics in animals raised for food.

And it also appears to me that the main thrust of the attack will be eliminating the use of antibiotics needed to maintain healthy animals in Concentrated Animal Feeding Operations, or CAFOs.

Eliminating antibiotics to control or prevent infections in our herds and flocks will eliminate many CAFOs and drive up the cost of protein to the point where many will have to look elsewhere for this portion of their diets. And many opponents of the use of antibiotics in animals say: "And that would be a good thing."

So is the agenda to protect me from multi-drug resistant bacteria, or is it to reduce the amount of animal products we consume?

To try and answer that question I want to supply the readers with some facts, facts that I will provide links for and can be repeated time after time as the truth, if anyone cares to listen to you.

A 2,500 pound prize bull with pneumonia is going to be treated with a much larger dosage of an antibiotic than an 8 pound newborn with the same bacterial infection.

A Look at the Numbers

First of all, a statistic often repeated by the crowd calling for change is that 80 percent of all antibiotics sold in the U.S. are used in animals.

The 80 percent number is meant to be a distraction from the real truth.

In truth, the numbers posted on the FDA's website, titled *2010 SUMMARY REPORT on Antimicrobials Sold or Distributed for Use in Food-Producing Animals,* are in total kilograms of drugs sold.

The listing is not indicative of what the antibiotics were used for, nor is it an accurate reflection of illnesses treated vs. prevented, etc.

For instance, a 2,500 pound prize bull with pneumonia is going to be treated with a much larger dosage of an antibiotic than an 8 pound newborn with the same bacterial infection.

But the numbers are the best we have for animal antibiotic use, so I will be using them today.

For human use of antibiotics, the same caveat about weight applies. The antibiotic numbers sold for human use that I will use for this discussion come from a letter to Congresswoman [Louise] Slaughter from the FDA dated April 19, 2011, citing the *IMS Health, IMS National Sales Perspectives data Year 2009.*

According to the FDA report, 28 percent of all antibiotics sold for animal use in 2010 were Ionophores. Ionophores have never been approved for use in human medicine.

Several other drugs sold for use in animals are also not approved for use in human medicine. When they are combined with the Ionophore total, the percentage of antibiotics sold for use in animals but having no place in human disease treatment reaches 45 percent.

Tetracycline Has Narrow Uses

The largest class overall of antibiotics sold or distributed for use in animals in 2010 was the tetracycline class. This class accounted for nearly 42 percent of total sales.

Tetracycline use in human medicine comprises about 1 percent of the total amount sold based on weight. Tetracycline used to be widely prescribed, but is now limited in use to treating the sexually transmitted disease caused by Chlamydia,

Mycoplasma infections and Rickettsial diseases like Lyme and Rocky Mountain Spotted Fever.

For these illnesses, there are antibiotics far superior to tetracycline. These other antibiotics, generally in the class called Macrolides, are the first line of therapy.

So the FDA statistics show that 87 percent of antibiotics used in animals are either never, or very rarely, used in human medicine.

Antibiotics critical to human health includes the cephalosporin and the fluoroquinolone classes. These two classes of antibiotics made up 24 percent of all human antibiotics sold in 2009, but combined, they only represented 0.3 percent of all antibiotics sold for use in animal health.

The reason for this disparity is that the FDA has already used its regulatory authority to limit these two categories of antibiotics to full therapeutic use to treat disease states in animals, limiting bacterial exposure to these antibiotics of critical importance to human health.

CAFOs did not contribute to this rapidly developing resistance. Human use did.

So when you read a report funded by the Pew Charitable Trust, or Consumers Union, stating that they found *Salmonella sp.* bacteria resistant to Cipro (a fluoroquinolone), where do you think that resistance came from? From the 11,000 kilograms used in animals, or from the 304,741 kilograms prescribed to treat humans?

Resistance Develops Quickly

Speaking of resistance in bacteria, penicillin was discovered in 1943; by 1950, just 7 short years later, 40 percent of all Staph isolates from US hospital intensive care units were resistant to penicillin. By 1960 that number was 80 percent.

Methicillin was discovered in 1959. In 1960 the first case of methicillin-resistant *Staphylococcus aureus* (MRSA) was found in England.

CAFOs did not contribute to this rapidly developing resistance. Human use did.

What about the other antibiotics of importance to human medicine, like penicillin and the aforementioned macrolide class? (An example of a macrolide, by the way, is the infamous Z-Pack, a front line drug for sinusitis and community acquired pneumonias, utilized in the past by many who will be reading this).

It is on these drugs that I think the discussion should be focused, realizing that the great majority of antibiotics used in animals are of little or no importance to me as a physician or grandparent, and that the two critical categories I mentioned above are already tightly regulated.

And the area of use that needs [to be] discussed is in the promotion category.

The FDA has approved four uses of antibiotics in animals: therapeutic, disease preventative, disease control and growth promotion through improved feed efficiency.

Congresswoman Slaughter's PAMTA [Preservation of Antibiotics for Medical Treatment Act] act and the proposals from many other organizations, well intended or not, would eliminate all antibiotic use in animals except for the treatment of actual infections, even though 87 percent of antibiotics used are not critical to your and my health.

Before anyone espouses such a radical change in policy, they should carefully review the statistics that followed Denmark's broad restrictions of antibiotic use in animals. The total amount of antibiotics prescribed for treating animal infections is up, and animal mortality is also up.

Which Is Worse?

When one treats an infection, not all the bacteria are always killed. Some survive by mutating and becoming antibiotic resistant.

I ask the question, "What produces more resistant bacteria—treating major infections with large dose, long term antibiotics, or with short term, low dose antibiotics to prevent the bacteria from multiplying in the first place?"

I don't have the answer, but someone had better find it before they potentially create an even worse problem through bad policy.

Because the FDA page does not clarify how many antibiotics are used for each category, we can only guess. And the best guesses I've seen come from the Animal Health Institute (AHI).

AHI estimates that somewhere around 12–15 percent are used in the growth promotion category.

[FDA] documents provide principles limiting the use of "medically important antibiotics" to judicious use only, [which] translated means for prevention, control and treatment.

Appropriately, this is where the FDA is focusing its latest efforts to keep our antibiotics working.

In June 2013, the FDA released its Guidance for Industry (GFI) 209, draft GFI 213 and the Veterinary Feed Directive proposed rule.

These documents provide principles limiting the use of "medically important antibiotics" to judicious use only, [which] translated means for prevention, control and treatment.

Injudicious use of these antibiotics important to human medicine [that] would be for performance (growth promotion), would voluntarily cease within three years and would be accompanied by a marketing status change from over the counter to prescription only.

The Infectious Diseases Society of America (IDSA), comprised of Infectious Disease specialists who consult on the most seriously infected patients, sent written testimony to FDA regarding the new Guidance for Industry documents, saying:

"IDSA commends FDA for moving forward with measures to encourage judicious use in animals of antimicrobials important to human health."

Voluntary vs. Mandatory Changes

A key caveat here is that the FDA is calling for this to be a voluntary change by the pharmaceutical industry and the men and women who grow our food-producing animals.

Many are not happy that the FDA did not take bigger, more aggressive steps.

Me personally, I think this erases my concerns—if industry and agriculture step up to the plate big time.

If they do not, we will hear even louder voices calling for a near total ban on antibiotics used in food-producing animals. And we may see the baby thrown out with the bath water.

Political pressure and political responses may produce change by legislation, not by rules and regulations, and there is a very important difference in the two methods of creating change.

When rules and regs are written in this country, they are usually written after lengthy debates and discussions amongst all parties, including scientists who review the facts.

Once written they are posted in the Federal Register with a 90-day comment period during which every American can say what is good or bad about the proposal, just as the IDSA did.

They are then either sent to OMB (The President) for review and approval or rejection, or they are rewritten based on the comments.

Two years to fruition is a fast tracked rule or regulation in this slow, deliberative process.

Legislation is often written behind closed doors, or appears as an amendment suddenly tucked onto a bill that simply must be passed, like an omnibus budget bill.

We saw that kind of political silliness when Congress moved catfish inspection over to the USDA in 2008.

And again when they barred USDA from implementing risk based inspection while mandating risk based inspection for FDA.

Biological Science vs. Political Science

I know which one I prefer, especially after having participated in both.

5

Hospitals Are a Primary Source of Superbug Infections

Michelle Castillo

Michelle Castillo is an associate editor for CBSNews.com.

Antibiotic-resistant superbug infections are on the rise nationwide, and more than twenty-three thousand Americans die each year from untreatable bacterial illnesses. Ironically, the biggest source of such deadly infections is hospitals themselves, which are beginning to recognize the seriousness of the problem and are taking steps to improve their practices. Many facilities are adopting antimicrobial stewardship programs to monitor and promote proper antibiotic use, while increased awareness of hygiene in health-care settings is helping reduce transmission, too. Some hospitals are also now making their infection rates public, which is good for patients and improves facility accountability.

The prevalence of antibiotic-resistant infections is increasing rapidly in the United States, according to a report released by the Centers for Disease Control and Prevention (CDC) on Monday [September 16, 2013].

More than two million people in the U.S. get drug-resistant infections annually. About 23,000 die from these diseases that are becoming increasingly resistant to antibiotics in doctors' arsenals.

"It is not too late," CDC director Dr. Tom Frieden said to CBSNews.com during a press conference. "If we're not careful,

Michelle Castillo, "CDC: Hospitals Major Source of Antibiotic-Resistant Infections," CBS News, September 16, 2013. Copyright © 2013 CBS News. All rights reserved. Reproduced with permission.

the medicine chest will be empty when we go there to look for a lifesaving antibiotic for someone with a deadly infection. If we act now, we can preserve these medications while we continue to work on lifesaving medications."

World Health Organization (WHO) Director-General Dr. Margaret Chan said in March 2012 that the overuse of antibiotics was becoming so common that she feared we may come to a day where any normal infection could become deadly because bacteria have evolved to survive our treatments.

The new report noted that antibiotic resistance costs $20 billion in excess health care costs in the U.S. each year, with costs to society for lost productivity reaching as much as an additional $35 billion.

Widely Prescribed

The CDC estimated in April that enough antibiotics are prescribed each year for four out of five Americans to be taking them. Doctors and other health care providers prescribed 258 million courses of antibiotics in 2010 for a population a little less than 309 million. They also estimated in this current report that up to 50 percent of antibiotics are prescribed incorrectly or to people who do not need them.

[CRE infections] are extremely resistant to even the strongest kinds of antibiotics, and can kill one out of every two patients who develop bloodstream infections caused by them.

Pediatricians have also urged doctors to avoid giving antibiotics unless it is absolutely necessary, especially for ear infections and sinusitis.

This is the first time the CDC has released statistics on which germs were most harmful. The antibiotic-resistant germs were designated either as urgent, serious or concerning. Researchers came up with the categories depending on how the germs impacted a person's health, the economic impact of the germ, how common the infection was, a 10-year projection of how dangerous the infection could become, how easily the germ spreads, how many antibiotics were available to treat it and how easy it infections can be prevented.

Carbapenem-resistant *Enterobacteriaceae* (CRE), drug-resistant gonorrhea and *Clostridium difficile* (C. diff), a serious infection typically caused by antibiotic use were all designated as urgent infections.

CRE Infections Are "Urgent"

CRE infections are caused by a family of 70 bacteria that normally live in the digestive system. They are extremely resistant to even the strongest kinds of antibiotics, and can kill one out of every two patients who develop bloodstream infections caused by them. Thirty-eight states reported at least one case of CRE last year, up from just one state a decade ago.

The CDC previously said in February that drug-resistant gonorrhea was on the rise, especially among men who have sex with men (MSM) living in the western U.S.

Though *C. diff* infections typically happen to older adults in hospitals or long-term care facilities after use of antibiotics, the Mayo Clinic reports that studies have shown that cases among people who are younger and healthier without having a history of antibiotic use or being near healthcare facilities are going up. The CDC report pointed out that *C. diff* causes about 250,000 hospitalizations and at least 14,000 deaths every year in the United States.

"We're getting closer and closer to the cliff," Dr. Michael Bell, deputy director of CDC's Division of Healthcare Quality Promotion, told reporters Monday.

Frieden said that the most acute source of antibiotic-resistant germs are hospitals, and urged facilities to take charge to prevent unnecessary illnesses. Antimicrobial stewardship programs, which measure and promote the correct use of antibiotics, have been shown to lower antibiotic-resistant infections in different facilities by as much as 80 percent.

"Every time antibiotics are used in any setting, bacteria evolve by developing resistance. This process can happen with alarming speed," Dr. Steve Solomon, director of CDC's Office of Antimicrobial Resistance, said in a press release.

Simple Prevention Measures

Frieden added that simple measures like making sure doctors wash their hands and checking that IVs and catheters—which are major sources of infection—only stay in as long as necessary can help reduce infection rates. He also pointed out that the CDC is encouraging hospitals to be transparent with their infection rates, and many websites now host that information for potential patients.

Bell added it is important that patients or family members are comfortable enough to ask questions if they feel something might be amiss.

The CDC also noted that some reports have shown that widespread use of antibiotics in food production have caused many resistant infections. The agency pointed out that the FDA has been pushing for responsible use of antimicrobials, and is telling producers to cut down on using the antibiotics for growth promotion in animals.

"We support appropriate antibiotic use," Bell said. "But, across the board there is always going to be bleedover in the environment and the ecosystem."

6

The Superbug MRSA Is Now Common in American Homes

Amy Norton

Amy Norton is a reporter for HealthDay, a news syndication service that focuses on health issues.

An antibiotic-resistant superbug that used to be found only in nursing homes and hospitals is now commonly found throughout the population, even in many American homes. Methicillin-resistant Staphylocossus aureus, *commonly known as MRSA, is spread by physical contact or by sharing items such as towels. Communal spaces such as locker rooms, prisons, and military barracks have long been prone to hosting MRSA, but recent research shows that the superbug is now "endemic" in American households as well. The study found that family members who lived with MRSA patients were frequently contaminated with the bacteria as well, as were the surfaces in their homes. MRSA strain USA300 is the main cause of community-acquired MRSA infections in the United States, and experts suspect inappropriate antibiotic use by humans has helped this particular drug-resistant strain develop.*

An antibiotic-resistant "superbug," long a problem in health-care settings, is now taking up residence in people's homes, a new U.S. study finds.

Methicillin-resistant *Staphylococcus aureus*, commonly referred to as MRSA, was once mainly confined to places like

Amy Norton, "Homes Now 'Reservoirs' for Superbug MRSA," HealthDay, April 21, 2014. HealthDay.com. Copyright © 2014 HealthDay. All rights reserved. Reproduced with permission.

hospitals and nursing homes, where it can cause severe conditions such as pneumonia and bloodstream infections.

But since the late 1980s, MRSA has also hit the wider community, where it usually causes skin infections, some of them potentially life-threatening. The bug is spread by skin-to-skin contact or through sharing supplies such as towels or razors. And certain groups are at increased risk, including athletes in contact sports and people living in cramped quarters, such as military barracks or prisons.

But in the new study, researchers found that such communal spaces are not the only major MRSA "reservoirs" out there.

"What our findings show is it's also endemic in households," said lead researcher Dr. Anne-Catrin Uhlemann, of Columbia University Medical Center in New York City.

[Researchers] found evidence that people's homes were "major reservoirs" of a MRSA strain called USA300— which is the chief cause of community MRSA infections across the United States.

MRSA is called a superbug because it is resistant to many common antibiotics. The new results, published April 21 [2014] in *Proceedings of the National Academy of Sciences*, are based on 161 New York City residents who contracted MRSA infections between 2009 and 2011.

Studying MRSA

Uhlemann's team analyzed the genetic makeup of MRSA samples from those patients, and took swabs from a comparison group of people the same age who had not fallen ill to see if they harbored any kind of *S. aureus* bacteria. The researchers also tested other members of each patient's household and their social contacts, and took samples from household surfaces to hunt for *S. aureus* contamination.

In the end, they found evidence that people's homes were "major reservoirs" of a MRSA strain called USA300—which is the chief cause of community MRSA infections across the United States.

Bacteria taken from people living in the same home, for example, were genetically very similar, while there was more genetic variability between samples from different households.

The implication, Uhlemann said, is that "we can't just treat the person with the infection. We have to attempt to remove the (MRSA) colonization from the home."

A MRSA expert who was not involved in the research said it "confirms what we've suspected all along."

"Transmission is a function of contact and time," said Dr. Henry Chambers, chair of the antimicrobial resistance committee for the Infectious Diseases Society of America. "At the end of the day, who are you in contact with the most? Your family."

If you have a MRSA infection, how do you protect your family members? "Basically, it boils down to keeping the wound covered, and frequent hand washing," Chambers said.

According to Uhlemann, you can also use bleach to clean surfaces, and hot water to wash bedding and clothes that an infected person has used. Chambers said the role of surfaces in transmitting MRSA is not "well delineated." But, he added, "it's good to clean."

Common Carriers

The U.S. Centers for Disease Control and Prevention estimates about one in three people carries staph bacteria in the nose, usually without sickness. About 2 percent of people harbor MRSA.

It's thought the superbug spread into the wider community because of antibiotic misuse and overuse. When bacteria are exposed to an antibiotic but survive, they can quickly mutate to become resistant to that drug.

Uhlemann's team found some more evidence to point the finger at antibiotic misuse. They discovered that mutations in USA300 that confer resistance to antibiotics called fluoroquinolones (such as ciprofloxacin, sold as Cipro) may have emerged around 1995 in New York City. Fluoroquinolone prescriptions would later soar nationwide—by about 50 percent between 1999 and 2008, the study says.

So it's possible that widespread use of those drugs helped the resistant USA300 strain spread.

"This, once again, argues for the careful use of antibiotics," Uhlemann said.

Chambers agreed. "We know that about half of antibiotics prescribed aren't needed," he said.

Antibiotics kill only bacteria, so they are useless against viral infections such as the common cold and should not be prescribed for those illnesses. If you do need an antibiotic, experts say it's important to take the full course. Stopping too soon could allow some bugs to survive and develop resistance to the drug.

Antibiotic Resistance Is a Global Public Health Threat

Honor Whiteman

Honor Whiteman is a staff writer for Medical News Today, *an online health-care publication.*

People don't just get sick or die from antibiotic-resistant bacteria in the United States; drug-resistant superbugs have spread around the globe and resistance in common bacteria has reached "alarming levels" in many parts of the world. Many infections that used to be handled by antibiotics, such as pneumonia, are now again potentially life threatening, and the World Health Organization warns that the world may be entering into a "post-antibiotic era" with devastating public health consequences. New antibiotics are urgently needed, but there is little financial incentive for drug companies to develop them since antibiotics are taken for a short duration, instead of being long-term money-makers for pharmaceutical companies.

"The time may come when penicillin can be bought by anyone in the shops. Then there is the danger that the ignorant man may easily underdose himself and by exposing his microbes to non-lethal quantities of the drug, make them resistant," said Alexander Fleming, speaking in his Nobel Prize acceptance speech in 1945.

As predicted almost 70 years ago by the man who discovered the first antibiotic, drug resistance is upon us.

Honor Whiteman, "Antibiotic Resistance: How Has It Become a Global Threat to Public Health?," medicalnewstoday.com, September 10, 2014. MedicalNewsToday.com. Copyright © 2014 Medical News Today. All rights reserved. Reproduced with permission.

A 2013 report from the Centers for Disease Control and Prevention (CDC) revealed that more than 2 million people in the US alone become ill every year as a result of antibiotic-resistant infections, and 23,000 die from such infections.

In April this year [2014], the World Health Organization (WHO) published their first global report on the issue, looking at data from 114 countries.

WHO focused on determining the rate of antibiotic resistance to seven bacteria responsible for many common infections, including pneumonia, diarrhea, urinary tract infections, gonorrhea and sepsis.

Their findings were worrying. The report revealed that resistance to common bacteria has reached "alarming" levels in many parts of the world, with some areas already out of treatment options for common infections.

For example, they found resistance to carbapenem antibiotics used to tackle *Klebsiella pneumoniae*—the bacteria responsible for hospital-acquired infections such as pneumonia and infections in newborns—has spread to all parts of the globe.

Although antibiotics have transformed modern medicine and have saved millions of lives over the years, their overuse has been a main driver of antibiotic resistance.

Dr. Keiji Fukuda, WHO's assistant director-general for health security, said of the report's findings: "Effective antibiotics have been one of the pillars allowing us to live longer, live healthier, and benefit from modern medicine. Unless we take significant actions to improve efforts to prevent infections and also change how we produce, prescribe and use antibiotics, the world will lose more and more of these global public health goods and the implications will be devastating."

In this spotlight feature, we look at what has contributed to antibiotic resistance since the drugs were discovered almost a century ago, and what is being done on a global scale to avoid falling into what WHO describes as a "post-antibiotic era."

Main Driver of Resistance

Antibiotics are drugs that slow down or destroy the growth of microorganisms, such as bacteria, fungi and parasites. Antibiotic resistance occurs when these microorganisms adapt to the drug that is attempting to attack it and continue to multiply in its presence.

Since the discovery of the first antibiotic—penicillin—in 1928, subsequent antibiotic discoveries moved at a rapid pace, particularly from the 1940s to 1980s. Some notable discoveries include cephalosporins—a class of antibiotics structurally related to penicillin—in 1948—carbapenems in 1976 and fluoroquinolones—antibiotics used to treat urinary tract infections—in 1980.

Dr. Steve Solomon, director of the CDC's Office of Antimicrobial Resistance, told *Medical News Today* that although antibiotics have transformed modern medicine and have saved millions of lives over the years, their overuse has been a main driver of antibiotic resistance. "During the last 70 years, bacteria have shown the ability to become resistant to every antibiotic that has been developed. And the more antibiotics are used, the more quickly bacteria develop resistance," he said.

The use of antibiotics at any time in any setting puts biological pressure on bacteria that promotes the development of resistance.

When antibiotics are needed to prevent or treat disease, they should always be used. But research has shown that as much as 50% of the time, antibiotics are prescribed when they are not needed or they are misused (for example, a patient is given the wrong dose). This inappropriate use of antibiotics unnecessarily promotes antibiotic resistance.

Poor Understanding

Dr. Charles Penn, coordinator of antimicrobial resistance at WHO, told *Medical News Today* that incorrect use of antibiotics is also a driver behind resistance.

"One of many reasons why antibiotic use is so high is that there is a poor understanding of the differences between bacteria, viruses and other pathogens, and of the proper use and value of antibiotics," he said.

"Antibiotics are very often prescribed for no useful purpose. Too many antibiotics are prescribed for viral infections such as colds, flu and diarrhea. Unfortunately, these public misconceptions are often perpetuated by media and others. For example, through the use of generic terms such as 'germs' and 'bugs.'"

He noted that dependence on antibiotics for modern medical benefits has contributed to drug resistance.

Excessive and incorrect use of antibiotics in food-producing animals has also been a key player in drug resistance.

"Surgery (elective and from trauma), cancer treatment (surgery and immunosuppressive therapy), intensive care generally, transplant surgery, even simple wound management would all become much riskier, more difficult options if we could not use antibiotics to prevent infection, or treat infections if they occurred," he said.

"Similarly, we now take it for granted that many infections are treatable with antibiotics, such as tonsillitis, gonorrhea and bacterial pneumonia. But some of these are now becoming unbeatable."

Excessive and incorrect use of antibiotics in food-producing animals has also been a key player in drug resistance, since resistant bacteria can be transmitted to humans through the food we eat.

Has Fleming's Warning Been Ignored?

We are now at a point where antibiotic resistance has become a serious threat to global public health. In a report earlier this year, Prof. Dame Sally Davies, chief medical officer for England, commented: "The soaring number of antibiotic-resistant infections poses such a great threat to society that in 20 years' time we could be taken back to a 19th century environment where everyday infections kill us as a result of routine operations."

But the threat of antibiotic resistance is not new. As stated previously, Fleming warned of the problem almost 70 years ago. According to Dr. Solomon, such warnings have been overlooked, particularly when the development of antibiotics was at its peak.

"Although many warnings about resistance were issued, prescribers became somewhat complacent about preserving the effectiveness of antibiotics—new drugs always seemed to be available," he told us. "However, the pipeline for discovery of new antibiotics has diminished in the past 30 years and has now run dry. As bacteria have evolved to resist our current drugs, doctors are now seeing patients with infections that are virtually untreatable."

He noted, however, that health care providers have now started to become more vigilant in prescribing antibiotics.

"Greater awareness of the urgency of the problem has given new impetus to careful stewardship of existing antibiotics. Prescribers are now heeding the warning that Fleming gave in his Nobel Prize acceptance speech—to use antibiotics judiciously or else lose them forever."

Dr. Penn disagrees that warnings of antibiotic resistance have been ignored, telling us that there has been a great deal of research and monitoring of the problem. "The issue has now become much more serious because the supply of new antibiotics is drying up," he added, "and despite the efforts of some, it is clear that antibiotic use globally is still rising fast."

The Barriers to Developing New Antibiotics

Looking back over the past 30 years, there has been astounding progression in the world of medicine. But despite this, there has been a significant decline in research and development of new antibiotics.

A 2004 report from the Infectious Diseases Society of America (IDSA), for example, found that between 1998 and 2002, approval from the Food and Drug Administration (FDA) for new antibiotics fell by 56%, compared with approval between 1983 and 1987. Furthermore, out of 89 new drugs approved by the FDA in 2002, none of them were antibiotics.

Antibiotics are short-course therapies, and companies know that they will make much more money selling a drug you have to take every day for the rest of your life.

As a result, we have been relying on the same antibiotics for decades, giving bacteria a better chance to evolve and develop resistance to them. In addition, we have been presented with an array of new infections that are already resistant to currently available antibiotics, such as methicillin-resistant *staphylococcus aureus* (MRSA).

The problem is that developing new antibiotics has become a more complex, costly and lengthy process. In a newsletter published by the Alliance for the Prudent Use of Antibiotics (APUA), Dr. Brad Spellburg, assistant professor of medicine at the University of California-Los Angeles (UCLA) and an author of the IDSA report, claims the "low-hanging fruit have been plucked" when it comes to identifying new antibiotics.

Economic Factors Play a Role

"Drug screens for new antibiotics tend to rediscover the same lead compounds over and over again," he said. "There have been more than 100 antibacterial agents developed for use in humans in the US since sulfonamides. Each new generation that has come to us has raised the bar for what is necessary to discover and develop the next generation."

He claims that economic factors have interfered with the development of new antibiotics. "The most obvious is that antibiotics are short-course therapies, and companies know that they will make much more money selling a drug you have to take every day for the rest of your life," he said, adding:

"Also, there are many types of infections, and approval for one type gets a company only one slice of the overall market pie. When antihypertensive drugs are approved, they are not approved to treat hypertension of the lung, or hypertension of the kidney. They are approved to treat hypertension. When antifungals are approved, they are approved to treat 'invasive aspergillosis,' or 'invasive candidiasis.'"

A Call for Global Action

Global leaders are in agreement that developing new antibiotics is one way to combat the problem of resistance. Earlier this year, UK Prime Minister David Cameron made a call for global action to tackle antibiotic resistance. Within this, he announced: "I have asked the economist Jim O'Neill to work with a panel of experts and report back to me and other world leaders on how we can accelerate the discovery and development of a new generation of antibiotics."

Last year, the US Department of Health and Human Services (HHS) announced it has formed an alliance with drug company GlaxoSmithKline in order to develop new drugs to combat both antibiotic resistance and bioterrorism.

"Working as strategic partners with a portfolio approach offers a new way to move forward in developing a robust pipeline of novel antibiotics that address gaps in our nation's preparedness as well as the evolving threat of antibiotic resistance," said Robin Robinson, PhD, director of the HHS' Biomedical Advanced Research and Development Authority.

Dr. Solomon told *Medical News Today*, however, that developing new antibiotics needs to be a continuous process in order to keep resistance at bay: "Because antibiotic resistance occurs as part of a natural process in which bacteria evolve, it can be slowed but not completely stopped. Therefore, new antibiotics always will be needed to keep up with resistant bacteria, as will new tests to track the development of resistance."

Developing new antibiotics alone will not tackle resistance. There needs to be a drastic change in the way antibiotics are prescribed by doctors and used by patients.

There has already been some progress in the creation of new antibiotics. We recently reported on a study by researchers from Japan who say a novel antibiotic—S-649266—has the potential to treat Gram-negative pathogens that are resistant to currently available antibiotics.

Earlier this year, a study from the University of East Anglia in the UK revealed a technique that could stop bacteria from becoming drug resistant. Co-author of this study Prof. Changjiang Dong told us: "This research provides the platform for urgently needed new generation drugs."

What Else Can Be Done?

But developing new antibiotics alone will not tackle resistance. There needs to be a drastic change in the way antibiotics are prescribed by doctors and used by patients, since this has been a key contributor to resistance.

WHO recommends that patients only use antibiotics when they are prescribed by a doctor. Furthermore, patients should take the full prescription, even if feeling better, and they should never share antibiotics with others or use leftover antibiotics.

When it comes to health care workers, WHO says they should only prescribe antibiotics when patients truly need them, and should ensure they are prescribing the correct antibiotic to treat the illness.

A key strategy to tackling antibiotic resistance lies in preventing infection in the first place. "Avoiding infections reduces the amount of antibiotics that have to be used and reduces the likelihood that resistance will develop," Dr. Solomon told us. "Drug-resistant infections can be prevented by immunization, infection prevention actions in health care settings, safe food preparation and handling and general handwashing."

The CDC [has] launched a series of campaigns to help educate health care professionals and the general public on the best ways to prevent infections and use antibiotics.

Detect and Protect

In addition, the organization launched an initiative called Detect and Protect against Antibiotic Resistance, which sets out four core actions that need to be addressed:

- Detect and track patterns of antibiotic resistance

- Respond to outbreaks involving antibiotic-resistant bacteria

- Prevent occurrence of infections and the spread of drug-resistant bacteria

- Discover new antibiotics and new diagnostic tests for drug-resistant bacteria.

Dr. Penn told *Medical News Today* that this year, WHO [has] the objective of developing a global action plan to address antibiotic resistance.

Building on the many recommendations, initiatives, and proposals over many years including from WHO, the Food and Agriculture Organization and the World Organisation for Animal Health, the aim of this global action plan is to bring these together so that a cohesive, multisectoral set of actions, can be implemented against an agreed set of measurable goals and targets.

A commitment to report progress against such goals and targets, by all countries, WHO and all other organizations and stakeholders is key to ensuring sustainable and effective action.

"We have been consulting widely on this plan," he continued, "including a web-based call for contributions which elicited more than 130 responses from national governments and their agencies, industry, consumer groups and other organizations including in animal health and agriculture. The draft global action plan will be submitted to WHO's Executive Board by the end of this year, and will be open for further consultation early next year before going to the World Health Assembly in May 2015."

Antibiotic resistance is a very real threat to public health and one that needs to be taken seriously. It seems global efforts to combat this threat are underway, but many health experts say such efforts need to produce results fast.

As Dr. Spellburg says: "If resistance to treatment continues to spread, our interconnected, high-tech world may find itself back in the dark ages of medicine, before today's miracle drugs ever existed."

8

Worldwide Country Situation Analysis: Response to Antimicrobial Resistance

World Health Organization

The World Health Organization (WHO) is an agency of the United Nations formed in 1948 with the goal of creating a world in which all people can enjoy both mental and physical health. The organization researches and endorses different methods of using antibiotics to combat diseases, and of monitoring antibiotic resistance.

Bacteria that are resistant to antibiotics have been found all over the world, and superbugs are one of the biggest threats to global public health today. Although most countries recognize the emergence of drug-resistant bacteria as urgent, few have taken significant steps to address the issue—some because they face other more pressing problems, such as regional conflicts, and others because they simply do not have the financial or scientific resources. Only a few countries have a national policy or strategy concerning antimicrobial resistance, and even some of the ones that do are not sufficiently prepared to tackle the issue. Public awareness on drug resistance remains low worldwide, an indication that superbugs are likely to continue developing and spreading.

World Health Organization, "Worldwide Country Situation Analysis: Response to Antimicrobial Resistance—Summary," WHO Press, April 2015. Reprinted from Publication Worldwide Country Situation Analysis: Response to Antimicrobial Resistance, World Health Organization, Summary. © 2015. All rights reserved. Reproduced with permission.

Antimicrobial resistance has been detected in all parts of the world; it is one of the greatest challenges to global public health today, and the problem is increasing. Although development of antimicrobial resistance is a natural phenomenon, its development and spread is being accelerated by misuse of antimicrobial medicines, inadequate or non-existent programmes for infection prevention and control, poor-quality medicines, weak laboratory capacity, inadequate surveillance and insufficient regulation of the use of antimicrobial medicines. A strong, collaborative approach will be required to combat antimicrobial resistance, involving countries in all regions and actors in many sectors.

Although widely recognized as an urgent problem by many international organizations and ministries of health, not all countries have a response plan to tackle antimicrobial resistance. Some regions face other, more pressing, problems and many low- to middle-income countries do not have the resources to implement response mechanisms.

Over a 2-year period, from 2013 to 2014, WHO [World Health Organization] undertook an initial "country situation analysis" in order to determine the extent to which effective practices and structures to address antimicrobial resistance have been put in place and where gaps remain. A survey was conducted in countries in all six WHO regions and focused on the building blocks that are considered prerequisites to combat antimicrobial resistance: a comprehensive national plan, laboratory capacity to undertake surveillance for resistant microorganisms, access to safe, effective antimicrobial medicines, control of the misuse of these medicines, awareness and understanding among the general public and effective infection prevention and control programmes.

Country authorities were asked to complete a questionnaire on their existing strategies, systems and activities. The questionnaires were completed either by the authorities themselves through self-assessment or at an interview with a WHO officer on the occasion of a country visit. A total of 133 of the 194 WHO Member States provided information.

Comprehensive national plans ... are regarded as one of the main ways to fight antimicrobial resistance globally; however, few countries reported having such a plan.

A full report is now available that presents the overall findings of the survey. The report provides an analysis, by region and globally, of the initiatives under way to address antimicrobial resistance and identifies areas in which more work is needed. This summary document provides an overview of the findings contained in the full report.

Since the survey was conducted, some countries have made further advances and additional initiatives have been launched. No reference therefore is made to individual countries, and the results reflect the situation at the time the questionnaires were completed.

National Plans and Other Strategies

Comprehensive national plans, based on a multisectoral approach and with sustainable financing, are regarded as one of the main ways to fight antimicrobial resistance globally; however, few countries reported having such a plan.

Other national mechanisms, such as a national focal point and a central coordination mechanism, were generally more common than plans. Many countries reported having a national policy or strategy, but few had published a progress report within the previous 5 years.

The findings from the survey indicate that progress in this area is needed in all regions, including in countries with strong health-care systems.

A national surveillance mechanism, based on well-equipped laboratories with well-trained staff that report regularly to functioning surveillance systems, allows the detection and tracking of antimicrobial-resistant microorganisms and enables prompt notification to the relevant authorities when an outbreak occurs. Surveillance can reveal the presence of patterns of resistant microorganisms and identify trends and outbreaks. Data from surveillance also allow policy-makers to introduce evidence-based standards and regulations and health care managers to make decisions on appropriate care.

The extent of surveillance of antimicrobial resistance reported in the survey varied by type of resistance and by country in all WHO regions. Regional networks support surveillance in many countries; however, none includes all the countries in its respective region.

Typically, countries cited a lack of laboratories with sufficient competent technical staff, weak infrastructure, poor data management and lack of standards as impediments to effective laboratory surveillance. Although laboratory capacity varied by country in all regions, at least one country in each of the six regions had a national reference laboratory capable of testing for antibiotic sensitivity and subject to external quality assessment. The same countries also reported monitoring of antimicrobial resistance in humans.

Both overuse and misuse of antimicrobial medicines accelerate the emergence of resistant microorganisms.

Access to Quality Assured Antimicrobial Medicines

Regions in which there are many high-income countries, such as the European and the Western Pacific regions, reported higher rates of access to high-quality medicines than other regions.

Ready access to quality-assured antimicrobial medicines is important for preventing the appearance of new antimicrobial-resistant microorganisms. Poor-quality medicines may not contain the correct amount of active ingredient, resulting in sub-optimal dosing. This can be overcome with strong national regulations on medicine production and by strengthening the ability of authorities to regulate the industry.

Counterfeit medicines have been reported to be a problem in many regions. The situation stems from weak regulatory systems and inability to enforce laws. The survey revealed that the wide availability of medicines for direct sale to patients—for example, on the Internet—remained a problem for all regions.

Use of Antimicrobial Medicines

Both overuse and misuse of antimicrobial medicines accelerate the emergence of resistant microorganisms. Misuse can be due to poor prescribing practice, including prescribing antimicrobial medicines when not required, incorrect choice of medicine, or at an incorrect dosage; self-medication in countries in which antimicrobial medicines are freely available; failure to finish a course of antimicrobial medicines or taking them for too long; lack of regulations or standards for health care workers; and misuse and overuse in animal husbandry and agriculture.

Many countries in all regions reported that antimicrobial medicines were generally freely available. However, few countries reported a system for monitoring the use of antimicrobial medicines; tracking of prescribing patterns and over-the-counter sales is therefore a significant challenge. The sale of antimicrobial medicines without prescription was widespread, and many countries lacked standard treatment guidelines for health care workers. Thus, overuse of antimicrobial medicines by the public and by the medical profession was a potential problem in all regions.

Public Awareness

At the time of the survey, public awareness appeared to be low in all regions. Even in some countries in which national public awareness campaigns had been conducted, there was still widespread belief that antibiotics are effective against viral infections. This situation is alarming, particularly in countries where antimicrobial medicines are readily available without a prescription.

Among professional groups, academics were generally more aware of the problem of antimicrobial resistance than others, including health care workers. The general lack of awareness in these sectors would indicate that antimicrobial resistance is likely to spread further. More education and collaborative awareness-raising campaigns in these sectors will be required. Without sufficient awareness, the appropriate regulations and standards will not be enacted, and other sectors will lack the information needed to implement them effectively.

Overall, the findings of this survey reveal that much is under way and indicate that countries are committed to addressing this complex problem.

Infection Prevention and Control Programmes

Resistant microorganisms can spread rapidly across countries, regions and the world, facilitated by global trade, travel and tourism. Poor infection control in any setting can greatly increase the spread of drug-resistant infections, especially during outbreaks of disease. Infection prevention and control programmes are thus essential to curb the movement of antimicrobial-resistant organisms, starting with good basic hygiene, which limits the spread of all infections, including those that are resistant to antimicrobial medicines.

Superbugs

Half the Member States in the European, South-East Asia and Western Pacific regions that responded to the survey reported having a national infection prevention and control programme; however fewer had corresponding programmes in place in all tertiary hospitals.

Overall, the findings of this survey reveal that much is under way and indicate that countries are committed to addressing this complex problem. Some countries already have a number of activities in place, while others are embarking on the work and face challenges. Nevertheless, increased efforts are needed in all regions, including in countries with strong health-care systems.

Five Strategic Objectives

Member States will review a draft global action plan on antimicrobial resistance at the Sixty-eighth World Health Assembly. The action plan sets out five strategic objectives: to improve awareness and understanding of antimicrobial resistance, to gain knowledge through surveillance and research, to reduce the incidence of infection, to optimize the use of antimicrobial medicines and to ensure sustainable investment in countering antimicrobial resistance.

It is anticipated that as countries continue to develop national action plans and to initiate effective practices and structure to address antimicrobial resistance, this initial country situation analysis will serve as a reference against which countries and WHO can monitor progress in meeting the challenge of antimicrobial resistance in coming years.

9

The United States Has a Plan to Combat Antibiotic Resistance

The White House

In March 2015, under the administration of Barack Obama, The White House issued the National Action Plan for Combating Antibiotic-Resistant Bacteria.

The United States recognizes the seriousness of antibiotic-resistant superbugs and has established an action plan to address the issue in a systematic and science-based way. The plan consists of five goals: 1) slow the emergence of resistant bacteria and prevent the spread of resistant infections; 2) strengthen surveillance and monitoring efforts to combat resistance; 3) advance the development and use of rapid diagnostic testing to identify resistant bacteria; 4) accelerate research and development of new antibiotics, vaccines, and other therapies; and 5) improve international collaboration and communication regarding prevention, monitoring, control, and research and development.

Antibiotics have been a critical public health tool since the discovery of penicillin in 1928, saving the lives of millions of people around the world. Today, however, the emergence of drug resistance in bacteria is reversing the miracles of the past eighty years, with drug choices for the treatment of many bacterial infections becoming increasingly limited, expensive, and, in some cases, nonexistent. The Centers for Disease Control

The White House, "National Action Plan for Combating Antibiotic-Resistant Bacteria," whitehouse.gov, March 2015. Courtesy of WhiteHouse.gov.

and Prevention (CDC) estimates that drug-resistant bacteria cause two million illnesses and approximately 23,000 deaths each year in the United States alone.

The *National Action Plan for Combating Antibiotic-Resistant Bacteria* provides a road map to guide the Nation in rising to this challenge. Developed in response to Executive Order 13676: Combating Antibiotic-Resistant Bacteria—issued by President Barack Obama on September 18, 2014—the *National Action Plan* outlines steps for implementing the *National Strategy for Combating Antibiotic-Resistant Bacteria* and addressing the policy recommendations of the President's Council of Advisors on Science and Technology (PCAST). Although its primary purpose is to guide activities by the U.S. Government, the *National Action Plan* is also designed to guide action by public health, healthcare, and veterinary partners in a common effort to address urgent and serious drug-resistant threats that affect people in the U.S. and around the world. Implementation of the *National Action Plan* will also support World Health Assembly resolution 67.25 (Antimicrobial Resistance), which urges countries to take urgent action at the national, regional, and local levels to combat resistance.

All of us who depend on antibiotics must join in a common effort to detect, stop, and prevent the emergence and spread of resistant bacteria.

The Goals of the *National Action Plan*

1. Slow the Emergence of Resistant Bacteria and Prevent the Spread of Resistant Infections.

2. Strengthen National One-Health Surveillance Efforts to Combat Resistance.

3. Advance Development and Use of Rapid and Innovative Diagnostic Tests for Identification and Characterization of Resistant Bacteria.

4. Accelerate Basic and Applied Research and Development for New Antibiotics, Other Therapeutics, and Vaccines.

5. Improve International Collaboration and Capacities for Antibiotic-Resistance Prevention, Surveillance, Control, and Antibiotic Research and Development.

By 2020, implementation of the *National Action Plan* will lead to major reductions in the incidence of urgent and serious threats, including carbapenem-resistant *Enterobacteriaceae* (CRE), methicillin-resistant *Staphylococcus aureus* (MRSA), and *Clostridium difficile*. The *National Action Plan* will also result in improved antibiotic stewardship in healthcare settings, prevention of the spread of drug-resistant threats, elimination of the use of medically-important antibiotics for growth promotion in food animals, and expanded surveillance for drug-resistant bacteria in humans and animals. Other significant outcomes include creation of a regional public health laboratory network, establishment of a specimen repository and sequence database that can be accessed by industrial and academic researchers, development of new diagnostic tests through a national challenge, and development of two or more antibiotic drug candidates or non-traditional therapeutics for treatment of human disease. In addition, the effort to combat resistant bacteria will become an international priority for global health security.

Task Force Will Monitor

Progress towards achieving these outcomes will be monitored by the U.S. Government Task Force that developed the *National Action Plan*. The Task Force, which is co-chaired by the Secretaries of Defense, Agriculture, and Health and Human Services, includes representatives from the Departments of

State, Justice, Veterans Affairs, and Homeland Security, as well as the Environmental Protection Agency, the United States Agency for International Development, the Office of Management and Budget, the Domestic Policy Council, the National Security Council, the Office of Science and Technology Policy, and the National Science Foundation. Additionally, the Presidential Advisory Council on Combating Antibiotic-Resistant Bacteria, created by Executive Order 13676, will provide advice, information, and recommendations to the Secretary of Health and Human Services regarding the *National Action Plan*'s programs and policies and their impact on the threat.

Implementation of the objectives and activities in the *National Action Plan* requires sustained, coordinated, and complementary efforts of individuals and groups around the world, including healthcare providers, healthcare leaders, veterinarians, agriculture industry leaders, manufacturers, policymakers, and patients. All of us who depend on antibiotics must join in a common effort to detect, stop, and prevent the emergence and spread of resistant bacteria. . . .

Aggressive action will move the nation towards major reductions in the incidence of urgent and serious drug-resistant threats.

The Plan's Vision and Scope

Antibiotics have been a critical public health tool since the discovery of penicillin in 1928, saving the lives of millions of people around the world. Today, however, the emergence of drug resistance in bacteria is reversing the gains of the past eighty years, with many important drug choices for the treatment of bacterial infections becoming increasingly limited, expensive, and, in some cases, nonexistent. The Centers for Disease Control and Prevention (CDC) estimates that each year at least two million illnesses and 23,000 deaths are caused by drug-resistant bacteria in the United States alone.

The loss of antibiotics that kill or inhibit the growth of bacteria means that we can no longer take for granted quick and reliable treatment of rare or common bacterial infections, including bacterial pneumonias, foodborne illnesses, and healthcare-associated infections. As more strains of bacteria become resistant to an ever larger number of antibiotics, we will also lose the benefits of a range of modern medical procedures—from hip replacements to organ transplants—whose safety depends on our ability to treat bacterial infections that may arise as post-surgical complications. Moreover, antibiotic-resistance also threatens animal health, agriculture, and the economy.

A Roadmap for the Nation

The *National Action Plan for Combating Antibiotic-Resistant Bacteria* provides a roadmap to guide the Nation in rising to this challenge. The *National Action Plan* outlines steps for implementing the *National Strategy for Combating Antibiotic-Resistant Bacteria* and addressing the policy recommendations of the President's Council of Advisors on Science and Technology. Although its primary purpose is to guide activities by the U.S. Government, the *National Action Plan* is also designed to guide action by public health, healthcare, and veterinary partners in a common effort to address urgent and serious drug-resistant threats that affect people in the U.S. and around the world.

Goals of the *National Action Plan*

The *National Action Plan* is organized around five goals for collaborative action by the U.S. Government, in partnership with foreign governments, individuals, and organizations aiming to strengthen healthcare, public health, veterinary medicine, agriculture, food safety, and research and manufacturing.

Aggressive action will move the nation towards major reductions in the incidence of urgent and serious drug-resistant threats, including carbapenem-resistant *Enterobacteriaceae* (CRE), methicillin-resistant *Staphylococcus aureus* (MRSA), and *Clostridium difficile*.

- Misuse and over-use of antibiotics in healthcare and food production continue to hasten the development of bacterial drug resistance, leading to loss of efficacy of existing antibiotics.

- Detecting and controlling antibiotic-resistance requires the adoption of a "One-Health" approach to disease surveillance that recognizes that resistance can arise in humans, animals, and the environment.

- Implementation of evidence-based infection control practices can prevent the spread of resistant pathogens.

- Interventions are necessary to accelerate private sector investment in the development of therapeutics to treat bacterial infections because current private sector interest in antibiotic development is limited.

- Researchers can use innovations and new technologies—including whole genome sequencing, metagenomics, and bioinformatic approaches—to develop next-generation tools to strengthen human and animal health, including:

  —Point-of-need diagnostic tests to distinguish rapidly between bacterial and viral infections as well as identify bacterial drug susceptibilities;

  —New antibiotics and other therapies that provide much needed treatment options for those infected with resistant bacterial strains; and

  —Antibiotic resistance is a global health problem that requires international attention and collaboration, because bacteria do not recognize borders.

Goal 1

Slow the Emergence of Resistant Bacteria and Prevent the Spread of Resistant Infections. Judicious use of antibiotics in healthcare and agricultural settings is essential to slow the emergence of resistance and extend the useful lifetime of effective antibiotics. Antibiotics are a precious resource, and preserving their usefulness will require cooperation and engagement by healthcare providers, healthcare leaders, pharmaceutical companies, veterinarians, the agricultural industry, and patients. Goal 1 activities include the optimal use of vaccines to prevent infections, implementation of healthcare policies and antibiotic stewardship programs that improve patient outcomes, and efforts to minimize the development of resistance by ensuring that each patient receives *the right antibiotic at the right time at the right dose for the right duration.* Prevention of resistance also requires rapid detection and control of outbreaks and regional efforts to control transmission across community and healthcare settings.

Improved diagnostics for detection of resistant bacteria ... will help healthcare providers make optimal treatment decisions and assist public health officials in taking action to prevent and control disease.

Goal 2

Strengthen National One-Health Surveillance Efforts to Combat Resistance. Improved detection and control of drug-resistant organisms will be achieved through an integrated, "One-Health" approach that includes the enhancement and integration of data from surveillance systems that monitor human pathogens—including the National Healthcare Safety Network (NHSN), the Emerging Infections Program (EIP), and the National Antimicrobial Resistance Monitoring System (NARMS)—with data from surveillance systems that monitor animal pathogens—including the National Animal Health Monitoring System (NAHMS), the National Animal Health Laboratory Network (NAHLN), and the Veterinary Laboratory Investigation and Response Network (Vet-LIRN). Goal 2 activities include creation of a regional public health laboratory network that provides a standardized platform for resistance testing and advanced capacity for genetic characterization of bacteria (e.g., through whole genome sequencing). Goal 2 activities will also enhance monitoring of antibiotic sales, usage, resistance, and management practices at multiple points along in the food-production chain, from farms to processing plants to supermarkets.

Goal 3

Advance Development and Use of Rapid and Innovative Diagnostic Tests for Identification and Characterization of Resistant Bacteria. Improved diagnostics for detection of resistant bacteria and characterization of resistance patterns will help healthcare providers make optimal treatment decisions and assist public health officials in taking action to prevent and control disease. Improved diagnostics will also help decrease unnecessary or inappropriate use of antibiotics. Goal 3 activities will accelerate the development of new diagnostics and expand their availability and use to improve treatment, enhance infection control, and achieve faster response to infections and outbreaks caused by resistant bacteria in hospitals and in the community.

Goal 4

Accelerate Basic and Applied Research and Development for New Antibiotics, Other Therapeutics, and Vaccines. Despite the urgent need for new antibiotics, the number of products in the drug-development pipeline is small and commercial interest remains limited. The advancement of drug development—as well as non-traditional therapeutics and vaccines—will require intensified efforts to boost scientific research, attract private investment, and facilitate clinical trials of new drug candidates. Goal 4 activities will help accomplish these objectives by supporting basic and applied research, providing researchers with scientific services (e.g., specimens, sequence data, and regulatory guidance), and fostering public-private partnerships that strengthen the clinical trials infrastructure and reduce the risks, uncertainty, and obstacles faced by companies who are developing new antibiotics and/or other therapeutics and vaccines that can impact the use of antibiotics and the development of resistance.

The National Action Plan *also supports World Health Assembly (WHA) resolution 67.25 (Antimicrobial Resistance), which . . . urges countries to develop and finance national plans and strategies and take urgent action at the national, regional, and local levels to combat resistance.*

Goal 5

Improve International Collaboration and Capacities for Antibiotic-Resistance Prevention, Surveillance, Control, and Antibiotic Research and Development. Antibiotic resistance is a worldwide problem that cannot be addressed by one nation in isolation. Goal 5 activities include working with foreign ministries of health and agriculture, the World Health Organization (WHO), the Food and Agriculture Organization (FAO), the World Organization for Animal Health (OIE), and other multinational organizations to enhance global capacity to detect, analyze, and report antibiotic use and resistance, create incentives for the development of therapeutics and diagnostics, and strengthen global efforts to prevent and control the emergence and spread of antibiotic-resistance. To advance these objectives, U.S. agencies will support development of a *WHO Global Action Plan on Antimicrobial Resistance,* enhance international collaborations including cooperation under the European Union-United States Trans-Atlantic Task Force on Antimicrobial Resistance (TATFAR), and mobilize global health resources through the Global Health Security Agenda.

How the Plan Was Developed

The *National Action Plan* was developed in response to Executive Order 13676: Combating Antibiotic-Resistant Bacteria, which was issued by President Barack Obama on September 18, 2014 in conjunction with the *National Strategy for Combating Antibiotic-Resistant Bacteria*.

The Executive Order calls for a U.S. Government Task Force to create a five-year action plan that lays out steps and milestones for achieving the *Strategy*'s goals and objectives and addressing the PCAST recommendations. The Task Force, which is co-chaired by the Secretaries of Defense, Agriculture, and Health and Human Services, includes representatives from the Department of State, the Department of Justice, the Department of Veterans Affairs, the Department of Homeland Security, the Environmental Protection Agency, the United States Agency for International Development, the Office of Management and Budget, the Domestic Policy Council, the National Security Council staff, the Office of Science and Technology Policy, and the National Science Foundation.

Development of the *National Action Plan* also supports World Health Assembly (WHA) resolution 67.25 (Antimicrobial Resistance), which was endorsed in May 2014 and urges countries to develop and finance national plans and strategies and take urgent action at the national, regional, and local levels to combat resistance. The resolution urges WHA Member States to develop practical and feasible approaches to, among other actions, extend the lifespan of drugs, strengthen pharmaceutical management systems and laboratory infrastructure, develop effective surveillance systems, and encourage the development of new diagnostics, drugs, and treatment options.

These recommendations are intended to inform the policy development process, and are not intended as a budget document. The commitment of resources to support these activities will be determined through the usual Executive Branch budget processes. Implementation of some of the actions in this report will require additional resources and these resources could be new or redirected from lower-priority Agency activities.

Monitoring and Evaluation

The Task Force created under Executive Order 13676 is charged with providing the President with annual updates on Federal Government actions to combat antibiotic resistance, including progress made in implementing the *National Action Plan*, plans for addressing obstacles and challenges, and recommendations for new or modified actions. The Presidential Advisory Council on Combating Antibiotic-Resistant Bacteria will provide advice, information, and recommendations to the Secretary of Health and Human Services regarding the programs and policies developed in the National Action Plan.

Implementation of the *National Action Plan* will require the sustained, coordinated, and complementary efforts of individuals and groups around the world, including public and private sector partners, healthcare providers, healthcare leaders, veterinarians, agriculture industry leaders, manufacturers, policymakers, and patients. All of us who depend on antibiotics must join in a common effort to detect, stop, and prevent the emergence and spread of resistant bacteria.

10

The US Government Is Not Doing Enough to Stop Superbugs

Tara Culp-Ressler

Tara Culp-Ressler is the health editor for ThinkProgress, *a blog site published by the Center for American Progress, a progressive public policy research and advocacy organization.*

Congress is not doing enough to protect the American public from the consequences of drug-resistant superbugs, even though it has had sufficient information and repeated opportunities to do so. Rep. Louise Slaughter (D-NY), a trained microbiologist, has been pushing for several years to restrict the use of antibiotics in food animals, but the farm and pharmaceutical industries still refute that there is a problem and have lobbied hard to stop her bill's passage every time. The Centers for Disease Control and Prevention warns that the United States faces "potentially catastrophic consequences" if the government does not take meaningful action to address the superbug issue.

Congress isn't taking any meaningful steps to protect Americans from the ever-increasing threat posed by antibiotic-resistant bacteria in the food industry, according to a new report issued on Tuesday [October 22, 2013]. Every recent legislative attempt to stem the use of antibiotics in animals has been blocked by the farm and pharmaceutical indus-

Tara Culp-Ressler, "The Growing Public Health Threat That Congress Isn't Doing Anything About," *ThinkProgress*, October 23, 2013. ThinkProgress.Org. Copyright © 2013 Center for American Progress. All rights reserved. Reproduced with permission.

tries—and public health researchers warn that's putting Americans at risk, even though the issue could easily be prevented with additional regulation.

If you don't understand why this is such a big deal, you're not alone. The rise of drug-resistant bacteria in meat has been a serious public health concern for years, but many Americans don't realize all of the factors at play.

Essentially, this is an issue that's been created by factory farming and the largely unregulated meat industry. When factory farms squeeze large numbers of animals into very tight quarters, that increases the risk that diseases will quickly spread among the livestock. To mitigate that risk, farmers pump their animals full of antibiotics—often, the exact same type of drugs that are given to sick humans. And, since antibiotics lose their effectiveness when they're overused, giving so many of them to animals threatens to increase drug-resistant bacteria strains. More than half of U.S. meat now contains bacteria that's resistant to antibiotics.

> In a couple of areas, the Obama administration started off with good intentions. But when industry pushed back, even weaker rules were issued.

The meat industry has maintained that using antibiotics in animals doesn't actually have a negative effect on people. But a mounting pile of evidence proves that wrong. One recent study demonstrated that drug-resistant bacteria in animals can be transferred to humans. And some factory farm workers have been revealed to be carrying antibiotic-resistant bacteria that originated in the animals they work with.

United States Lags Behind Other Countries

Other countries ban the practice of giving antibiotics to animals for non-medical purposes. But the United States hasn't taken any steps in that direction—in fact, we currently don't even require farmers to report the types or the quantities of drugs they're using on livestock. Tuesday's new report, issued by the Johns Hopkins Center for a Livable Future, points out that regulation in this area has actually regressed under the [President Barack] Obama administration.

"In a couple of areas, the Obama administration started off with good intentions. But when industry pushed back, even weaker rules were issued," Bob Martin, executive director of the Center for a Livable Future, told the *Washington Post.* "We saw undue influence everywhere we turned."

The report was released five years after a landmark study, also conducted by scientists at Johns Hopkins, first reported about the pressing need to curb antibiotics in animals. Back then, public health researchers warned that continuing the practice would give rise to drug resistance. Now, Martin says, "our worst fears were confirmed."

An "Antibiotic Apocalypse"

At a panel assembled by Johns Hopkins to discuss the results of the report, experts expressed skepticism that U.S. Congress will actually take any real steps to address this issue, and laid the blame at the feet of "the political power of industrial agriculture." For instance, Rep. Louise Slaughter (D-NY) has been pushing for legislation to give the government more oversight over this area of the food industry for years. But her initiatives are repeatedly stalled.

Public health officials don't mince words when they discuss the risk of growing drug resistance. Earlier this year, medical experts in England warned that the increasing prevalence of drug-resistant diseases will eventually lead to an "antibiotic apocalypse"—a time in the not-so-distant future when people will die from infections because there aren't any drugs left to treat them. Researchers at the Centers for Disease Control recently warned that the U.S. faces "potentially catastrophic consequences" if we don't move to address this issue.

And at Tuesday's panel, a researcher from the Harvard School of Public Health noted that the risk to our health is "real and immediate" and we will eventually see "common infections become fatal."

Leaders in the livestock industry, on the other hand, said the new Johns Hopkins report is simply a "scaremongering attack."

Race Against Time to Develop New Antibiotics

Theresa Braine

Theresa Braine is a freelance journalist who has reported exten-sively for the Bulletin of the World Health Organization.

There isn't much incentive for pharmaceutical companies to de-velop new antibiotics to fight drug-resistant strains of bacteria. The research and development expenses are high and the profit return is low because antibiotics are taken for a short time and they cure the illness they are meant to treat, rather than being taken for many years to manage a chronic condition, which is how drug companies make most of their money. Only five major drug companies were researching new antibacterial drugs by 2008. Because the free market is not inclined to solve the super-bug problem, combating drug-resistant bacteria must become an urgent global priority and the drug company profit-motive must be somehow removed in order for it to happen.

Within a few days of scraping his leg in a scooter accident in 2009, nine-year-old Brock Wade was in hospital fighting for his life with a methicillin-resistant *Staphylococcus aureus* (MRSA) infection. Once the infection—caused by one of the bacteria most often resistant to antibiotics—had been diagnosed, doctors put him on five different antibiotics. "After a month in the hospital, and against all odds, Brock recovered

Theresa Braine, "Race Against Time to Develop New Antibiotics," *Bulletin of the World Health Organization*, March 2, 2011. Copyright © 2011. All rights reserved. Reproduced with permission.

and was well enough to come home," says his mother Rhonda Bailey-Wade on the web site of the Infectious Diseases Society of America (IDSA).

Scenarios such as this IDSA case study are increasingly being played out all over the world. But not all the thousands of patients that contract drug-resistant bacterial infections every year are as lucky as Brock. And the problem looks set to get worse. While infectious agents are becoming more and more resistant to the medicines that are currently in use, not enough drugs are being developed to combat them.

"MRSA continues to be a major cause of community-acquired antibiotic resistant infections," says Dr Brad Spellberg, one of the authors of the 2004 IDSA report *Bad bugs no drugs*. "However, because companies in the late 1980s and early 1990s recognized the threat of MRSA, starting in 2000 we did get new MRSA drugs. Right now, we have reasonable antibiotics to treat MRSA. As resistance catches up with them, in the future we will have problems again."

There are many reasons. One is scientific. "The low-hanging fruit has been picked," says Spellberg. "But the concept that we've exhausted the pantry is ridiculous. Now we have to dig deeper, think harder and more cleverly."

A comprehensive study of antibiotic development . . . found in 2008 that only 15 antibiotics of 167 under development had a new mechanism of action with the potential to meet the challenge of multidrug resistance.

Another reason is commercial. Antibiotics, in particular, have a poor return on investment because they are taken for a short period of time and cure their target disease. In contrast, drugs that treat chronic illness, such as high blood pressure, are taken daily for the rest of a patient's life. "Companies have figured out that they make a lot more money selling the latter drugs than they do selling antibiotics," Spellberg says, highlighting the lack of incentive for companies to develop antibiotics.

That's why many companies have stopped developing antibiotics altogether. Only five major pharmaceutical companies—albeit five of the biggest—GlaxoSmithKline, Novartis, AstraZeneca, Merck and Pfizer, still had active antibacterial discovery programmes in 2008, according to an article published in the journal *Clinical Infectious Diseases* in January 2009.

Adding to the grim picture, a comprehensive study of antibiotic development, covering innovative, small firms, as well as pharma giants, found in 2008 that only 15 antibiotics of 167 under development had a new mechanism of action with the potential to meet the challenge of multidrug resistance. Most of those were in the early phases of development, according to the study entitled *The Bacterial Challenge: Time to React*.

But there is hope. "Given that the antibiotics we have available today were discovered as growth byproducts of bacteria that we can culture, and that we've cultured less than 1% of the bacteria on our planet, there are many potential solutions out there," Spellberg says.

A variety of biological solutions have yet to be fully explored, such as phage therapy and the potential use of the lytic enzymes found in mucus and saliva to kill pathogens (as described by researchers in an article published in October 2010 in the Institute of Physics' journal *Physical Biology*).

Another example is that of researchers at GlaxoSmithKline who recently described a novel class of antibacterial agents that target type IIA topoisomerases. The article was published in *Nature* in August 2010. "This investigational compound class has activity against a broad spectrum of Gram-positive and Gram-negative bacteria," says Dr Mick Gwyn, the study's lead author and a researcher in antibacterial drug discovery at GlaxoSmithKline.

Antimicrobial resistance is the inevitable consequence of prescribing antibiotics. "Whatever infections we treat, the bacteria that are part of our normal flora are always exposed to these antibiotics," says Dr Hajo Grundmann, chair of infectious diseases and epidemiology at the University of Groningen and head of the Department of Bacteriology at the National Institute of Public Health in the Netherlands. "Simply by surviving the onslaught of antibiotics, they are developing more clever ways to overcome the most sophisticated and advanced antibiotics."

There are no global data on the number of cases, including fatal ones, of resistant bacterial infections. According to the 2008 study, every year at least 25,000 patients in the European Union alone die from an infection caused by multidrug-resistant bacteria and estimated additional health-care costs and productivity losses are at least 1.5 billion Euros.

We're starting to see virtually or totally pan-resistant bacteria spilling into the community.

Some of the most resistant infections are caused by Gram-negative *Acinetobacter*, and by certain strains of *Klebsiella* and *Pseudomonas* species, according to Spellberg. These bacteria cause a variety of illnesses ranging from hospital-acquired pneumonia, bloodstream infections, urinary tract infections from catheters, abdominal infections and even meningitis in people who have had head and spine procedures, for example, epidurals during labour.

"Anywhere in the body can be hit by these bugs. And the issue is that without effective antibiotics the death rate is much higher," says Spellberg.

The outbreak of resistant strains of *Escherichia coli (E. coli)*—a common cause of food poisoning—carrying a gene called NDM1 (New Delhi metallo-β-lactamase) in India in 2010, which spread to other countries, is a case in point. Until recently such completely resistant bacteria have only been found in hospitals, Spellberg says, but "now we're starting to see virtually or totally pan-resistant bacteria spilling into the community."

The solution may lie not only in scientific discovery but also in the economic incentives for developing drugs. "I think that Congress understands that this is now a market failure and that economic incentives are needed to correct the market failure," he says.

Public-private partnerships could provide one solution, according to a May 2010 commentary in the *British Medical Journal*, such as the GlaxoSmithKline research partnerships with the Wellcome Trust and with the United States Defence Threat Reduction Agency.

Referring to "the twin challenges of conserving the effectiveness of existing antibacterial drugs and developing new ones," authors of the *British Medical Journal* article Anthony So, Melissa Furlong and Andreas Heddini of Swedish-based nongovernmental organization, ReAct, write that "delinking research and development costs from drug pricing and the return that drug companies receive on investment could correct misaligned economic incentives."

This delinking of research costs and drug pricing is something that industry may be prepared to accept, according to Richard Bergström, director-general of LIF, the trade association for the research-based pharmaceutical industry in Sweden.

"Incentives that separate the financial return from the use of a product are the only way to change this behaviour," said Bergström at a conference held at Uppsala University in September 2010. "Intelligent pull incentives, such as advance commitments and prizes, provide financial rewards to the developer that are not based on the volume of use of the novel antibiotic. With the right set-up, pharma companies will have no incentive to drive use. Maybe they will not do any promotion at all. Use would be agreed with public policymakers, purchasers and national health systems."

Bergström called for a "global compact" similar to the one used for the United Nations programme for good governance and sustainable development enshrined in Millennium Development Goal 7. This agreement "could focus on the agreed and gradual introduction—and responsible marketing and use of—new agents."

"A global compact would require that not only industry but also governments, physicians and pharmacists join forces to preserve the new medicines that our children and grandchildren need," said Bergström. "No single tool will solve the problem. What is really needed is a collection of incentives that address the multiple obstacles to success."

12

Superbug Outbreaks Prompt Calls for Mandatory Reporting

Chad Terhune

Chad Terhune covers health care for the Los Angeles Times.

Recent superbug outbreaks in two Los Angeles-area hospitals are "just the tip of the iceberg" when it comes to antibiotic-resistant infections that represent an urgent public health threat. Moreover, the incidents involving carbapenum-resistant Enterobacteriaceae *(CRE) illustrate the need for a nationwide reporting system so officials can monitor and track illnesses and deaths caused by a wide variety of resistant bacteria. The Los Angeles outbreaks—which could have been far worse if not for the vigilance of health officials—have prompted calls for mandatory nationwide reporting. Currently, only two superbugs (not including CRE) are reportable at the federal level; twenty states have their own superbug reporting requirements, and several take part in a voluntary reporting program run by the Centers for Disease Control and Prevention.*

Well before the recent superbug outbreaks at UCLA and Cedars-Sinai hospitals, federal health officials had labeled deadly CRE [carbapenum-resistant *Enterobacteriaceae*] bacteria an urgent threat.

Yet there are still no national reporting requirements for the antibiotic-resistant superbug, and only 20 states have imposed any rules. California is not among them.

Chad Terhune, "Superbug Outbreaks Prompt Calls for Mandatory Reporting," *Los Angeles Times*, March 6, 2015. Copyright © 2015 Los Angeles Times. All rights reserved. Reproduced with permission.

When L.A. County officials examined the problem in 2011, they found 675 cases of CRE among patients at hospitals, nursing homes and long-term acute-care facilities over a one-year period.

Those cover a broader set of CRE infections, beyond just those from tainted hospital scopes that are grabbing attention now. The number of patients affected is probably far greater, experts say, and increasingly worrisome.

The incidents at UCLA and Cedars are "just the tip of the iceberg," said Dr. Benjamin Schwartz, deputy chief of the acute communicable disease control program at the L.A. County Department of Public Health. "It's really a problem that is much more widespread."

Now outbreaks across the nation have prompted calls for mandatory reporting to stem the spread of CRE and to make the public more aware of the risks.

The stakes are high. With few treatment options, CRE can be fatal in up to half of infected patients.

"It's important to know what's out there, because these are serious infections," said Peter Mendel, a researcher and expert on infection reporting at Rand Corp., a Santa Monica think tank. "You shouldn't wait until there's an outbreak."

A Push for Legislation

Rep. Ted Lieu (D-Los Angeles) said he plans to introduce legislation soon requiring hospitals to report CRE cases to the Centers for Disease Control and Prevention (CDC).

"I don't see how we can combat superbugs if the CDC doesn't even know the full scope of the problem," Lieu said. "We should have uniform national reporting for all hospitals."

The stakes are high. With few treatment options, CRE can be fatal in up to half of infected patients.

On Wednesday [March 4, 2015], Cedars-Sinai Medical Center disclosed that four patients were infected with CRE from a contaminated scope. Seven people were sickened by CRE at UCLA's Ronald Reagan Medical Center.

A spokeswoman for the CDC said reporting requirements are generally set at the state level so "ultimately the decision should be based on what makes sense for prevention in a particular state."

In 2013, the CDC labeled CRE an urgent threat, and director Tom Frieden has called it a "nightmare bacteria."

But at the federal level, two other deadly germs have received far more attention. Officials already require reporting of MRSA, or methicillin-resistant *Staphylococcus aureus*, and *Clostridium difficile*, a bacterium that can cause deadly bouts of diarrhea.

Alternate Strategies

There are other approaches to take beyond mandatory reporting, infection-control experts say. In Illinois, for instance, the state runs a registry of CRE-infected patients so hospitals and other medical providers can know whether a highly contagious patient requires isolation and other precautions to be taken.

The CRE fight is at a crucial moment.... There are concerns about the bacteria spreading in the wider community without stronger preventive measures.

Health officials can periodically survey hospital lab data for CRE, and hospitals can conduct routine monitoring of high-risk areas such as intensive-care units.

There are many ways patients can be exposed to CRE. It's often spread by contaminated medical equipment and on the hands of healthcare workers.

Health officials say the CRE fight is at a crucial moment. It's largely confined to healthcare settings for now, but there are concerns about the bacteria spreading in the wider community without stronger preventive measures.

With that in mind, L.A. health officials are gearing up for a new round of CRE surveillance backed by $1.5 million in federal grant money.

The most recent county study dates to 2011, and it discovered a CRE outbreak of 24 cases at a 177-bed long-term-care facility over a two-month period. Those details were published in a 2013 medical journal article.

Incomplete Details

Schwartz said the county doesn't name facilities that report cases or release information on patients. There weren't details available on the outcome for patients overall.

Thirteen of those patients in the outbreak were sent to other hospitals for further treatment of their infections, according to the county. If not for its surveillance, officials acknowledged, the outbreak would probably have gone unreported.

Those 24 CRE cases were part of the 675 overall for a one-year period ending in May 2011.

"We had a lot more of it than we thought," said Dr. Dawn Terashita, a medical epidemiologist with the county.

Two-thirds of the 102 acute-care hospitals analyzed had at least one case. The infection rate was significantly higher inside the eight long-term-care facilities reviewed.

Schwartz said those long-term-care patients often bounce in and out of the hospital, carrying the bacteria with them.

In the aggregate, infected patients tended to be older and more female.

L.A. County is one of eight public health agencies across the country, including ones in New York and Oregon, taking part in the CDC program on CRE surveillance.

For that new program, county officials said they are considering whether to require medical facilities to submit CRE cases versus take voluntary reports. Schwartz said 27 hospitals have already agreed to share data.

"We want to understand how this resistant bacteria is transmitted between different parts of the healthcare system," he said. "It may give us some good clues on what we can do to prevent transmission."

13

Congress Hesitant to Move on Curbing Antibiotic Use in Livestock

Robert King

Robert King is a health-care correspondent for the Washington Examiner.

As a trained microbiologist, congresswoman Louise Slaughter (D-NY) understands the perilous link between antibiotic use in livestock and antibiotic resistance in humans. That is why Slaughter introduced legislation in 2015 to ban medically important antibiotics from being used in livestock feed for nontherapeutic uses, such as to promote weight gain. It was the fifth time that she submitted such a bill. Her legislation has been stalled each time due to intense lobbying from the agribusiness and pharmaceutical industries, which wield considerable power in the halls of Congress. Slaughter is optimistic that as consumers become increasingly informed about the superbug issue, there will be more pressure on her fellow representatives to move such a bill forward.

McDonald's, Costco and Chick-fil-A are curbing their use of chickens raised on antibiotics due to rising concerns from the American public that consuming such meat and poultry can foster drug resistance.

Congress, however, isn't likely to act on the issue.

Robert King, "Congress Hesitant to Move on Curbing Antibiotic Use in Livestock," *Washington Examiner*, March 26, 2015. WashingtonExaminer.com. Copyright © 2015 Washington Examiner. All rights reserved. Reproduced with permission.

Rep. Louise Slaughter, D-N.Y., reintroduced on Tuesday [March 24, 2015] for the fifth time legislation to curb antibiotic use in livestock. The bill stalled every time after pushback from agribusiness, who use the drugs to help their livestock grow and keep the animals well, and pharmaceutical companies that sell the antibiotics to farmers and ranchers.

However, Slaughter, a microbiologist, believes that her bill has a better chance of passing now that the general public is more aware of the link between antibiotic use in livestock and antibiotic resistance in humans.

A 2012 poll of 1,000 U.S. residents conducted by *Consumer Reports* found 86 percent of consumers indicated that meat raised without antibiotics should be in their local supermarket.

"The people of the United States are really understanding what is going on here more than the House of Representatives," Slaughter told the *Washington Examiner*.

The Centers for Disease Control and Prevention [CDC] has said excessive antibiotic use in animals could create resistance in humans.

Building Resistance

If antibiotics are used too much, [bacteria] could build up a resistance to it. That resistant bacteria can remain on animal meat and, when not cooked properly, spread to humans, according to the CDC.

Slaughter's bill would ban eight classes of medically important antibiotics, such as penicillin and tetracycline, from being used to help livestock get bigger.

It isn't just through consumed meat. Fertilizer or water containing animal waste and drug-resistant bacteria are used on crops, and the bacteria in the animal waste can remain on the crops and be eaten, CDC said.

Another source of antibiotic resistance is overprescribing by doctors.

The agency estimates that at least 23,000 people die each year from drug-resistant infections.

Slaughter's bill would ban eight classes of medically important antibiotics, such as penicillin and tetracycline, from being used to help livestock get bigger. The antibiotics could still be used to treat sick animals.

However, the legislation is completely unnecessary, as farmers already are moving to reduce antibiotic use to grow animals, said Dave Warren, spokesman for the National Pork Producers Council.

Voluntary Guidelines from FDA

Next year, an FDA [Food and Drug Administration] regulatory guidance will go into effect that says medically important antibiotics shouldn't be used to enhance growth. Medical use of the drugs would require veterinary oversight.

The Animal Health Institute, which is funded by the pharmaceutical industry, also highlighted the FDA guidance.

"When fully implemented, medically important antibiotics will be used only to fight disease under the supervision of a veterinarian," the institute told the *Examiner*.

Slaughter said the FDA's guidance is only voluntary, and contains a loophole that allows antibiotic use for prevention of illnesses—a loophole that her bill would close. Warren countered that if farmers can't use antibiotics to prevent illnesses, then it will result in more sick animals.

"Would you rather have meat from an animal that was sick or one that was healthy?" he asked.

Warren also noted that there are no studies that definitively link antibiotic use in livestock to antibiotic-resistant treatment failures in people.

A source tells the *Examiner* that the House Energy and Commerce Committee, to which Slaughter's bill was referred, doesn't have any plans to take up [the] legislation.

While Slaughter was optimistic, she wouldn't be surprised if the fifth time wasn't the charm.

"This is not a Congress that has a great scientific background or in many cases believes in it," she said. "I don't expect anybody is going to be jumping to bring up this bill."

14

Antibacterial Products May Actually Promote Antibiotic Resistance

Kiera Butler

Kiera Butler is a senior editor at Mother Jones *magazine.*

Antibacterial soap products are popular with germ-phobic consumers, but they may do more harm than good when it comes to antibiotic-resistant bacteria, especially if they contain an antimicrobial agent called triclosan. Triclosan, which is an ingredient in everything from soaps to socks to yoga mats, has been linked to the development of antibiotic resistance and has also been found to contaminate waterways and disrupt hormones in lab animals. Experts say that products containing antibacterial chemicals like triclosan are not necessary and that good old fashioned hand washing with soap and water or an alcohol-based hand sanitizer is much better.

To hear the industry tell it, anti-microbial soaps are humanity's last best option in a war against germs that lurk everywhere. On a site called Fight Germs Now—"the official source on anti-bacterial hygiene products"—the American Cleaning Institute sings their praises, warning that "sometimes plain soap and water is not good enough." The fast-growing market for anti-bacterials—most of which rely on an active ingredient called triclosan—is estimated at $1 billion.

Kiera Butler, "Does Purell Breed Superbugs?," *Mother Jones*, January/February 2014. Copyright © 2014 Mother Jones Magazine. All rights reserved. Reproduced with permission.

Triclosan is also in items such as socks, yoga mats, cutting boards, ice cream scoops, and pencils. No wonder the Centers for Disease Control and Prevention (CDC) estimates that it's present in the urine of three-quarters of Americans.

But on December 16 [2013], the FDA [Food and Drug Administration] issued a proposed rule that would require companies to provide "more substantial data to demonstrate the safety and effectiveness of antibacterial soaps" before selling these products. The move is in response to the mounting evidence that triclosan might not be as effective as manufacturers claim. Bill Schaffner, a professor of preventive medicine and infectious diseases at Vanderbilt University, points out that triclosan soap products are useless when it comes to most seasonal infections: They target bacteria, not the viruses that cause colds and flus. And they don't work any better on bacteria than standard soap—which also gets rid of viruses. In a 2008 review in the *American Journal of Public Health*, researchers scrutinized hundreds of hand hygiene studies and found "little evidence" that anything beat regular washing in reducing the symptoms associated with infectious gastrointestinal or respiratory illnesses.

The public health implications of triclosan led the European Union to ban it in 2010 from any product that might come into contact with food.

Triclosan Is a Trigger

Not only that, but there is strong evidence that anti-bacterial soaps contribute to antibiotic resistance. In 2004, a team of University of Michigan researchers found that exposing bacteria to triclosan increased activity in cellular pumps that the bugs use to eliminate foreign substances. These overactive excretory systems "could act to pump out other antibiotics, as well," says Stuart Levy, one of the study's authors and a leading researcher on antibiotic resistance at the Tufts University School of Medicine. That's a problem, since troublesome bacteria like streptococcus, staphylococcus, and pneumonia are already evolving defenses against our best weapons. Worse, there aren't enough new drugs in the production pipeline. Over the past 15 years, the FDA has approved just 15 new antibiotics—in the preceding 15 years, it approved 40. The World Health Organization now views antibiotic resistance as "a threat to global health security." And while triclosan's contribution to the problem hasn't been adequately studied, Levy believes it could be "significant."

Triclosan also gets into waterways, where it could harm aquatic life. A 2013 Loyola University simulation found that the chemical caused "dramatic" algae die-offs and altered the natural composition of bacteria in streams—a potential problem for higher species, including vulnerable frogs and salamanders. Other recent studies have found that triclosan disrupts hormone production in lab animals.

Lawmakers Take Note

The public health implications of triclosan led the European Union to ban it in 2010 from any product that might come into contact with food. Two years later, Johnson & Johnson pledged to phase it out entirely. The Food and Drug Administration was supposed to deliver a ruling on the chemical's safety in 2012, but it still hasn't completed its review. Meanwhile, with traces of the stuff showing up in Minnesota lakes, lawmakers there are pushing what would be the nation's first triclosan ban.

After learning about all of this, I was worried I might have to abandon my habit of squirting Purell all over my hands every time I get off the subway. But there's no triclosan in Purell. In fact, most hand sanitizers rely on alcohol, which slays germs on contact instead of killing some and just weakening others, as the anti-bacterials do. Vanderbilt's Schaffner assures me that alcohol-based hand sanitizers "will absolutely not contribute to the problem of antibiotic resistance, since they are not antibiotics."

Elaine Larson, an associate dean for research at Columbia University's School of Nursing who has led dozens of studies on hand hygiene, argues that sanitizers can be more effective than soap and water, whose efficacy in removing germs depends on how thoroughly you wash. "If I wanted to clean my hands fast, I would use an alcohol-based hand sanitizer," Larson says. The CDC agrees: In its guidelines for health care workers, it notes that "alcohol-based solutions were more effective than washing hands with plain soap in all studies."

Regular Hand-Washing Is Still Best

Note, though, that alcohol doesn't remove actual dirt—which is why the CDC recommends regular soap and water as the best all-around option outside hospital settings. And hand sanitizer won't work against the stomach bug norovirus or the armored spores of *C. difficile*, a serious and sometimes life-threatening infection most often found in hospitals: "You literally have to wash the spores off your hands and flush them down the sink," Schaffner says. But for virtually all other germs, alcohol is very effective. "During flu season I am in favor of abundant use of alcohol-based hand sanitizers," he says.

So if you're a germophobe like me, it doesn't hurt to grab a bottle of Purell for the road, but you might consider ditching those anti-bacterials. Contrary to industry spin, most of the time, plain old soap and water is good enough.

15

From a Medieval Text, a Weapon Against a Modern Superbug Emerges

Melissa Healy

Melissa Healy covers health and science for the Los Angeles Times *newspaper and website.*

A recently discovered wound remedy from the Middle Ages could hold a key to the development of new drugs to fight antibiotic-resistant superbugs. Researchers duplicated the recipe from a one-thousand-year-old Viking text and found that it killed not only regular staph bacteria but also Methicillin-resistant Staphylocossus aureus, *commonly known as the superbug MRSA. When it didn't kill the germs, it disrupted how they communicate with each other, which could prove to be a key mechanism of action in the development of future medications. Researchers were especially stunned by the discovery because the effective wound remedy predated the scientific discovery of germ theory.*

At the University of Nottingham in Britain, researchers have rediscovered an ancient medicinal elixir that appears to fight a very modern scourge: a deadly drug-resistant bacterial infection rampant in hospitals.

The discovery melds medieval potion-making with modern pharmacology. In its crosshairs: Methicillin-resistant *Staphylococcus aureus*, better known as MRSA.

Melissa Healy, "From a Medieval Text, a Weapon Against a Modern Superbug Emerges," *Los Angeles Times*, March 31, 2015. LATimes.com. Copyright © 2015 Los Angeles Times. All rights reserved. Reproduced with permission.

Let's imagine that during a nighttime escape through Sherwood Forest, an early archetype for the legendary figure Robin Hood scratched his cornea on a branch and developed an eye infection. In nearby Nottingham, he might well have consulted an herbalist, who would fetch a brass vessel, brew a remedy of bile from a cow's stomach and Allium—a plant from the garlic family—and create an unguent to treat the patient's inflamed eye.

Until recently, the recipe for that medieval remedy lay unnoticed in the brittle pages of a 1,000-year-old text—titled *Bald's Leechbook*—shelved in the library of the University of Nottingham's Institute for Medieval Research.

Leafing through that folio, Viking studies professor Christina Lee wondered what its ancient recipes revealed about the state of medieval medical knowledge, and whether and how, a millennium before the germ theory of disease was understood, healers and herbalists had guessed right in choosing their treatments.

The 1,000-year-old recipe had a powerful killing effect: roughly 1 in 1,000 bacterial cells growing in plugs of collagen survived when doused with the ancient salve.

Lee translated the recipe for the eye salve from the original Old English recipe in *Bald's Leechbook* and enlisted chemists at her university's Center for Biomolecular Sciences to recreate the unguent and test its effect.

Lee's request came at a crucial time. With a paucity of new antimicrobial medications in the development pipeline, Nottingham microbiologist Freya Harrison was looking for inspiration. Lee's idea might allow her team to reach deep into the past in search of undiscovered or underappreciated antimicrobial agents.

Following the Ancient Recipe

Scientists in Harrison's lab followed the recipe precisely, making four separate batches with fresh ingredients each time. They also devised a control treatment using the same quantity of distilled water and brass sheet to mimic the brewing container, but leaving the vegetable compounds out.

In lab conditions that set off riotous growth of the *Staphylococcus aureus* bacteria, the 1,000-year-old recipe had a powerful killing effect: roughly 1 in 1,000 bacterial cells growing in plugs of collagen survived when doused with the ancient salve.

Later, in infected wounds induced in mice, the remedy killed 90% of MRSA bacteria.

Harrison says she was "absolutely blown away" with the antique recipe's effects. She had assumed it might show "a small amount of antibiotic activity." Researchers have found some of its elements—copper and bile salts in particular—to have some effect on bacteria in the lab. And plants in the garlic family are known to make chemicals that interfere with bacteria's ability to damage infected tissues.

But compared with the control substance, there was something powerful about the combination of these elements in this ancient formulation, Harrison said. The eye salve had the power even to breach the sticky coating and the dense clustering of mature colonies of bacteria, which are notoriously resistant to antibacterial treatments.

Mechanism of Action Uncovered

When Harrison's lab diluted the salve to see whether it would continue to work, they perceived what they believe is the medication's mechanism of action: Even when the diluted salve failed to kill *S. aureus*, it interfered with communication among cells in the bacterial colony—a key finding because those signals switch on genes that allow bacteria to damage infected tissues. Blocking this signaling is seen as a promising way to treat infection.

"We know that MRSA-infected wounds are exceptionally difficult to treat in people and in mouse models," said Kendra Rumbaugh, who performed the testing of Bald's remedy on MRSA-infected skin wounds in mice. "We have not tested a single antibiotic or experimental therapeutic that is completely effective," added Rumbaugh, a professor of surgery at Texas Tech University's School of Medicine. But she said the ancient remedy was at least as effective—"if not better than the conventional antibiotics we used."

The collaboration between Old English remedies and microbiology has given rise to a program called AncientBiotics at Nottingham, where researchers will seek funding to extend research combining the ancient arts and modern sciences.

Organizations to Contact

The editors have compiled the following list of organizations concerned with the issues debated in this book. The descriptions are derived from materials provided by the organizations. All have publications or information available for interested readers. The list was compiled on the date of publication of the present volume; the information provided here may change. Be aware that many organizations take several weeks or longer to respond to inquiries, so allow as much time as possible.

Alliance for the Prudent Use of Antibiotics (APUA)
136 Harrison Ave., M&V Suite 811, Boston, MA   02111
(617) 636-0966 • fax: (617) 636-3999
e-mail: apua@tufts.edu
website: www.tufts.edu/med/apua

Headquartered on the campus of Tufts University Medical School in Boston, the Alliance for the Prudent Use of Antibiotics (APUA) is a nonprofit organization that has chapters in more than sixty countries. It is dedicated to containing antibiotic resistance and improving antibiotic effectiveness through research, education, capacity building, and global and grassroots advocacy. APUA's website features a wide variety of research reports, advocacy letters, news articles, reviews, external links, and an archive of the group's quarterly newsletter.

Centers for Disease Control and Prevention (CDC)
1600 Clifton Rd., Atlanta, GA   30333
(800) 232-4636
website: www.cdc.gov

Founded in 1946, the Centers for Disease Control and Prevention (CDC) was originally charged with the task of finding methods to control malaria. The organization's mission has broadened since its inception, but it still focuses on preventing and managing both communicable and noncommunicable diseases. The CDC offers guidelines for professionals and the general public on how to reduce the spread of antibiotic-resistant bacteria. The CDC website features a variety of fact sheets and articles on antibiotic use and preventing the development of resistant bacteria strains. Titles of interest include "About Antibiotic Use and Resistance," "Get Smart About Antibiotics," and "Antibiotic Resistance and Food Safety."

Food and Water Watch (FWW)
1616 P St. NW, Suite 300, Washington, DC   20036
(202) 683-2500 • fax: (202) 683-2501
e-mail: info@fwwatch.org
website: www.foodandwaterwatch.org

Founded in 2005, Food and Water Watch (FWW) is a nonprofit organization that advocates for policies that will result in healthy, safe food and access to safe and affordable drinking water. The organization believes that it is essential for shared resources to be regulated in the public interest rather than for private gain, and it strongly opposes the use of antibiotics in animal feed. The organization's website devotes a special section to the topic of antibiotic use, featuring issue briefs, fact sheets, and reports with titles such as "Save Antibiotics for Medicine, Not Factory Farms," "What FDA Can't Tell Us About Antibiotic Use in Animals," and "Playing Catch-up with Superbugs."

National Institutes of Health (NIH)
9000 Rockville Pike, Bethesda, MD   20892
(301) 496-4000
e-mail: NIHinfo@od.nih.gov
website: www.nih.gov

Founded in 1887, the National Institutes of Health (NIH) is one of the world's foremost medical research centers as well as the federal focal point for medical research in the United States. The NIH, which comprises twenty-seven separate institutes and centers, is one of eight health agencies of the Public Health Service, which in turn is part of the Department of

Health and Human Services. Resources available on the NIH website include dozens of reports related to superbugs and antibiotic resistance, such as "Antibiotic Resistance—Why Is the Problem So Difficult to Solve?," "Antibiotic Resistance as a Global Threat," and "On the Trail of Drug-Defying Superbugs."

Natural Resources Defense Council (NRDC)
40 West 20th St., New York, NY 10011
(212) 727-2700 • fax: (212) 727-1773
e-mail: nrdcinfo@nrdc.org
website: www.nrdc.org

The Natural Resources Defense Council (NRDC) promotes the international protection of wildlife and wild places through law, science, and the activism of more than a million members. Some of the group's main focuses include climate change, alternative energy, and protection of the world's oceans and endangered habitats. The NRDC website offers in-depth information about antibiotic resistance, including hundreds of articles, reports, blog posts, and FAQs. Titles of interest include "Billions of Enemy Soldiers," "Food Safety Concerns from Antibiotic Resistance—No Better, Maybe Worse," and "Antibiotic Resistance, Antibiotic Stewardship."

Union of Concerned Scientists (UCS)
2 Brattle Square, Cambridge, MA 02138-3780
(617) 547-5552 • fax: (617) 864-9405
website: www.ucsusa.org

The Union of Concerned Scientists (UCS) is a membership organization of citizens and scientists who work together to promote the responsible use of science to improve the world. UCS has extensively researched and reported on the use of antibiotics in animal feed, and the group supports legislation to reduce the use of antibiotics in food animals. Resources available on the UCS website include "Prescription for Trouble: Using Antibiotics to Fatten Livestock," "The Mounting Scientific Case Against Animal Use of Antibiotics," and a template via which site visitors are invited to contribute their own stories about encounters with antibiotic-resistant bacteria.

US Department of Agriculture (USDA)

1400 Independence Ave. SW, Washington, DC   20250
(202) 720-2791
website: www.usda.gov

The US Department of Agriculture (USDA) is the federal government agency responsible for developing and executing US farm policy. The USDA website includes news updates, reports, and publications such as the *Agriculture Fact Book*. The website's search engine returns nearly five thousand results for the term "antibiotic resistance," including the full text of the department's *2015 Antimicrobial Resistance (AMR) Plan* and many articles about antibiotic use in agriculture.

US Food and Drug Administration (FDA)

10903 New Hampshire Ave., Silver Spring, MD   20993-0002
(888) 463-6332
website: www.fda.gov

The US Food and Drug Administration (FDA) is the federal government agency responsible for ensuring the quality and safety of all food and drug products sold in the United States. The FDA's website includes a wide variety of congressional testimony, reports, and articles about superbugs and antibiotic resistance, including "Battle of the Bugs; Fighting Antibiotic Resistance," "Recent Developments in Combating Antibiotic Resistance," and "Educational Resources; Antibiotics and Antibiotic Resistance." An FDA podcast on antibiotic resistance may be of particular interest and is available on the site.

The White House

1600 Pennsylvania Ave. NW, Washington, DC   20500
(202) 456-1111
website: www.whitehouse.gov

Whitehouse.gov is the website of the president of the United States, Barack Obama. Resources available from the site include presidential statements and speeches about antibiotic resistance, in-depth fact sheets, statistical reports, essays, news articles, press releases, blogs, and links to other useful resources. Publications of particular interest include the full text of the *National Action Plan for Combating Drug-Resistant Bacteria* and information about the White House Forum on Antibiotic Stewardship.

World Health Organization (WHO)
Avenue Appia 20, Geneva 27   CH-1211
 Switzerland
+41 22 791 21 11 • fax: +41 22 791 31 11
e-mail: info@who.int
website: www.who.int

The World Health Organization (WHO) is an agency of the United Nations formed in 1948 with the goal of creating and ensuring a world in which all people can live with high levels of both mental and physical health. The organization researches and endorses different methods of using antibiotics to combat diseases, such as tuberculosis, and of monitoring antibiotic resistance. WHO publishes the *Bulletin of the World Health Organization*, which is available online, and the *Pan American Journal of Public Health*. WHO's website contains a library of WHO reports and publications, as well as links to various world health journals and reports. Superbug-related publications include "Mobilizing Political Will to Contain Antimicrobial Resistance" and "WHO's First Global Report on Antibiotic Resistance Reveals Serious, Worldwide Threat to Public Health," among others.

Bibliography

Books

Gus Barrett — *The MRSA Book: Guide to MRSA Treatment, Identification and Prevention.* Seattle: Amazon Digital, 2014.

Delene Bartie — *Antibiotics: History, Science, and Issues (The Story of a Drug).* Westport, CT: Greenwood, 2015.

Martin Blaser — *Missing Microbes: How the Overuse of Antibiotics Is Fueling Our Modern Plagues.* New York: Picador, 2015.

Karl Drlica and David Perlin — *Antibiotic Resistance: Understanding and Responding to an Emerging Crisis.* Upper Saddle River, NJ: FT Press Science, 2011.

Philip Lymbery and Isabel Oakeshott — *Farmageddon: The True Cost of Cheap Meat.* New York: Bloomsbury USA, 2014.

Maryn McKenna — *Superbug: The Fatal Menace of MRSA.* New York: Free Press, 2010.

Ola Sköld — *Antibiotics and Antibiotic Resistance.* Hoboken, NJ: Wiley, 2011.

Brad Spellberg — *Rising Plague—The Global Threat from Deadly Bacteria and Our Dwindling Arsenal to Fight Them.* New York: Prometheus, 2009.

Beverly Williams   *MRSA the X Factor: The Super Guide to the Super Bug.* Seattle: Amazon Digital, 2014.

Periodicals and Internet Sources

Coco Ballantyne   "Hospitals and Superbugs: Go in Sick . . . Get Sicker," *Scientific American,* October 18, 2007.

BBC News   "Superbugs 'Spread by Hospital Wet Wipes,'" June 8, 2015. www.bbc.com.

Mark Bello   "A 'Superbug' Resistant to Most Antibiotics," *The Legal Examiner,* February 19, 2015. http://farmingtonhills.legalexaminer.com.

Sarah Boseley   "New Wave of 'Superbugs' Poses Dire Threat, Says Chief Medical Officer," *Guardian* (UK), March 10, 2013.

Centers for Disease Control and Prevention   "Antibiotic Threats in the United States, 2013," 2013. www.cdc.gov.

Centers for Disease Control and Prevention   "Mission Critical: Preventing Antibiotic Resistance," April 24, 2014. www.cdc.gov.

Centers for Disease Control and Prevention   "Untreatable: Report by CDC Details Today's Drug-Resistant Health Threats," September 16, 2013. www.cdc.gov.

Alicia Chang and John Rogers   "Lawyer: Teen Infected by 'Superbug' Struggling to Survive," Associated Press, February 20, 2015. http://apnews.myway.com.

Elizabeth Cohen   "CRE Outbreak: You're Due to Go in for a Procedure. Should You Be Worried?," CNN, February 20, 2015. www.cnn.com.

Elizabeth Cohen   "Deadly Superbug-Related Scopes Sold Without FDA Approval," CNN, March 5, 2015. www.cnn.com.

Tara Culp-Ressler   "Four Ways That Superbugs Are Already Threatening Public Health," *ThinkProgress*, October 30, 2013. www.thinkprogress.org.

Caroline Smith DeWaal and Susan Vaughn Grooters   "Antibiotic Resistance in Foodborne Pathogens," Center for Science in the Public Interest, May 2013. http://cspinet.org.

Jovana Drinjakovic   "The War Against Superbugs: Can Drug-Resistant Bacteria Be Beaten?," *Globe and Mail*, April 5, 2015.

Peter Eisler   "Deadly 'Superbugs' Invade US Health Care Facilities," *USA Today*, March 6, 2013.

Lorenzo Ferrigno   "Why Scientists Are Studying Germ Universe in NY Subway," CNN, February 19, 2015. www.cnn.com.

Caitlyn Fitzpatrick   "Alarming WHO Report Reveals Inadequate Global Efforts to Combat Antibiotic Resistance," *MD Magazine*, April 30, 2015. www.hcplive.com.

Tom Frieden — "Antibiotic Resistance Threats: Many Countries Have Inadequate Plans to Tackle Antibiotic Resistance, WHO Finds," *Pharmaceutical Journal*, May 2015. www.pharmaceutical-journal.com.

Jerome Groopman — "Superbugs: The New Generation of Resistant Infections Is Almost Impossible to Treat," *New Yorker*, August 11, 2008.

Terry Gross — "Antibiotics Can't Keep up with 'Nightmare' Superbugs," National Public Radio, October 22, 2013. www.npr.org.

Infection Control Today — "Experts Say Antibiotic Resistance Has Potential to Undermine Healthcare, Create 'Apocalyptic Scenario,'" 2013. www.infectioncontroltoday.com.

Alexander Kaufman — "Antibiotic Use in Meat Is Soaring," *Huffington Post*, March 21, 2015. www.huffingtonpost.com.

Brent Kim et al. — "Industrial Food Animal Production in America: Examining the Impact of the Pew Commission's Priority Recommendations," Johns Hopkins Center for a Livable Future, Fall 2013. www.jhsph.edu/research /centers-and-institutes/johns-hopkins -center-for-a-livable-future.

Anthony King and Chemistry World — "Antibiotic Resistance Will Kill 300 Million People by 2050," *Scientific American*, December 16, 2014.

Brian Krans — "Antibiotic Resistance: Why Our Best Medical Weapon Is Losing Its Edge," *Healthline*, July 24, 2014. www.healthline.com.

Brian Krans — "Politics Stall Antibiotics Ban in Congress," *Healthline*, July 24, 2014. www.healthline.com.

Nicholas Kristof — "Our Pigs, Our Food, Our Health," *New York Times*, March 11, 2009.

Vivian Kuo and Dana Ford — "Superbug Cases Reported in North Carolina; 1 Dead," CNN, February 23, 2015. www.cnn.com.

Sandee LaMotte — "Obama Battles 'Superbugs' with National Plan," CNN, March 27, 2015. www.cnn.com.

Losee Ling et al. — "A New Antibiotic Kills Pathogens Without Detectable Resistance," *Nature*, January 22, 2015.

Kevin Liptak — "White House Wants $1.2 Billion to Combat 'Superbugs,'" CNN, January 27, 2015. www.cnn.com.

Kevin Loria — "Everyone Has the Hand Sanitizer Story Wrong," *Business Insider*, April 25, 2014.

Mayo Clinic — "Antibiotics: Misuse Puts You and Others at Risk," December 12, 2014. www.mayoclinic.org.

Maryn McKenna   "'Catastrophic Threat': UK Government Calls Antibiotic Resistance a 'Ticking Time Bomb,'" *Wired*, March 11, 2013. www.wired.com.

Maryn McKenna   "Your McNuggets: Soon Without a Side of Antibiotics," *Wired*, March 4, 2015. www.wired.com.

Joseph Mercola   "FDA Fails to Protect Against Antibiotic Resistance, Guarantees More Needless Death and Suffering," mercola.com, April 23, 2014. http://articles.mercola.com.

Natural Resources Defense Council   "Food, Farm Animals and Drugs," 2015. www.nrdc.org.

Amy Nordrum and Elizabeth Whitman   "Antibiotic Resistance: How Livestock Lobbyists and Drug Companies Hinder the US Fight Against Superbugs," *International Business Times*, April 29, 2015.

Kim O'Donnel   "7 Cities Pass Resolutions Urging Congress to Ban Unnecessary Antibiotics in Meat," *Civil Eats*, April 14, 2014. http://civileats.com.

Jim O'Neill   "Antimicrobial Resistance: Tackling a Crisis for the Health and Wealth of Nations," *Review on Antimicrobial Resistance*, December 2014.

Jim O'Neill   "How Big Pharma Can Save Antibiotics from Superbugs," *Wired*, May 15, 2015. www.wired.com.

PEW Charitable Trusts   "Antibiotic Resistance and Food Animal Production: A Bibliography of Scientific Studies (1969–2014)," 2014. www.pewtrusts.org.

Nedra Pickler   "White House Unveils Plan to Fight Antibiotic-Resistant Germs," Associated Press, March 27, 2015. http://apnews.myway.com.

Brad Plumer   "The FDA Is Cracking Down on Antibiotics on Farms. Here's What You Should Know," *Washington Post*, December 14, 2013.

Jordan Rau   "UCLA Outbreak Highlights Challenge of Curbing Infections," National Public Radio, February 20, 2015. www.npr.org.

Ben Rooney   "Tyson to Phase out Antibiotics in Chicken," CNN/Money, April 28, 2015. http://money.cnn.com.

Ian Sample   "Antibiotic-Resistant Diseases Pose 'Apocalyptic' Threat, Top Expert Says," *Guardian* (UK), January 23, 2013.

Susan Scutti   "Antibiotic-Resistant Bacteria from American Cattle Become Airborne, but Is It Life-Threatening?," *Medical Daily*, March 30, 2015. www.medicaldaily.com.

Ed Silverman   "Can the US Really Curtail Antibiotic
                      Use in Livestock and Thwart
                      Superbugs?," *WSJ Pharmalot*, April 3,
                      2015. http://blogs.wsj.com.

Louise Slaughter   "The Demise of Modern Medicine,"
                      Medium, March 23, 2015.
                      https://medium.com.

Mike Stobbe   "Imported Drug-Resistant Stomach
                      Bug Spreading in US," Associated
                      Press, March 2, 2015.
                      http://hosted.ap.org.

Chad Terhune   "Superbug Linked to 2 Deaths at
                      UCLA Hospital; 179 Potentially
                      Exposed," *Los Angeles Times*, February
                      19, 2015.

Chad Terhune   "Superbug Outbreak Extends to
                      Cedars-Sinai Hospital, Linked to
                      Scope," *Los Angeles Times*, March 4,
                      2015.

Nick Thompson   "Thousand-Year-Old Anglo-Saxon
and Laura   Potion Kills MRSA Superbug," CNN,
Smith-Spark   March 31, 2015. www.cnn.com.

US Government   "Agencies Have Made Limited
Accountability   Progress Addressing Antibiotic Use in
Office   Animals," 2011. http://gao.gov.

The White House   "Fact Sheet: President's 2016 Budget
                      Proposes Historic Investment to
                      Combat Antibiotic-Resistant Bacteria
                      to Protect Public Health," January 27,
                      2015. www.whitehouse.gov.

World Health Organization Advisory Group on Integrated Surveillance of Antimicrobial Resistance (AGISAR)

"Critically Important Antimicrobials for Human Medicine, 3rd Revision," 2011. http://apps.who.int.

Lydia Zuraw

"Rep. Slaughter Reintroduces Preservation of Antibiotics Legislation," *Food Safety News*, March 25, 2015.

Index

A

World Health Organization (WHO)
- antibiotic resistance, 13, 29, 45, 53, 61
- antimicrobial resistance, 62–68, 101
- introduction, 9

World Organization for Animal Health (OIE), 61, 77

Z

Z-Pack drug, 40